D0758308

THE CLAUSTRUM

THE CLAUSTRUM

An Investigation of Claustrophobic Phenomena

DONALD MELTZER

WITH AN ESSAY BY MEG HARRIS WILLIAMS
Macbeth's Equivocation, Shakespeare's Ambiguity

The Clunie Press
for
The Roland Harris Trust Library
No. 15

© The Roland Harris Education Trust

First published 1992

All rights reserved. No part of this publication may be reproduced, stored in a retrieval system, or transmitted, in any form or by any means, electronic, mechanical, photocopying, recording, or otherwise, without the prior permission of The Roland Harris Education Trust.

British Library Cataloguing in Publication Data

Meltzer, Donald, 1922 -
The claustrum: an investigation of claustophobic phenomena. — (The Roland Harris trust library; no.15)
I. Title   II. Series
616.85225

ISBN 0 902 965 298

Typeset by Action Typesetting Limited, Gloucester
Printed and bound in Great Britain by
Billing & Sons Ltd, Worcester

THE CLAUSTRUM

An Investigation of Claustrophobic Phenomena

Donald Meltzer

with an essay by Meg Harris Williams

Contents

Part One

	Introduction	3
Chapter 1	Melanie Klein's Vision of Projective Identification	7
Chapter 2	Review of Earlier Publications	13

Part Two

Chapter 3	The Geographic Dimension of the Mental Apparatus	57
Chapter 4	The Compartments of the Internal Mother	61
Chapter 5	Life in the Claustrum	69
Chapter 6	Technical Problems of the Claustrum	97

Part Three

Chapter 7	Emergence from the Claustrum versus shift of Consiousness	111
Chapter 8	The Role of the Claustrum in the Onset of Schizophrenia	117
Chapter 9	Concerning the Ubiquity of Projective Identification	127
Chapter 10	Symptomatology versus Characterology – The Psycho-analytical Process	135
Chapter 11	The Claustrum and Adolescence	143
Chapter 12	The Claustrum and the Perversions/Addictions	149
Chapter 13	The Claustrum and Politics	153
Addendum	Macbeth's Equivocation, Shakespeare's Ambiguity (*Meg Harris Williams*)	159

Part 1

Introduction

Together with these harmful excrements, expelled in hatred, split-off parts of the ego are also projected on to the mother, or, as I would rather call it, *into* the mother. These excrements and bad parts of the self are meant not only to injure but also to control and take possession of the object. Insofar as the mother comes to contain the bad parts of the self she is not felt to be a separate individual but is felt to be *the* bad self.

("Notes on Some Schizoid Mechanisms")

The thrust of psycho-analysis has moved relentlessly from a simplistic explanatory hypothesis and an optimistic aim to cure mental illnesses, towards a state of bewildered description of mental phenomena. In its tremulous hope of doing more good than harm, both appelations — schizoid and mechanism — have fallen away from our use of the terms splitting processes and projective identification. First of all neither of them are confined to what Melanie Klein called the paranoid-schizoid position, and secondly they are of a different level of abstraction in the vocabulary of psycho-analysis. Splitting processes is a way of describing something that must happen to account for the fluctuations in the integration of self and objects. Projective identification, on the other hand, is the name of an omnipotently implemented phantasy affecting the relationships between parts of the self and objects in the external and internal worlds.

This book is an attempt to bring together my clinical experiences of the operation of projective identification as seen in the consulting room, and from this to extrapolate a view of it as a mental phenomenon of significance in the development of the individual and in the evolution of the society that each person both inhabits and in some measure helps to form. It is over forty years since Mrs. Klein's modestly presented paper marked the watershed between her early amplification of Freud and Abraham's model of the mind and the later Kleinian and Post-Kleinian developments. Certainly her following of Freud's bold dismantling of the concept of unity of the mind has played an important role; but the progress in these decades has been characterized above all by the exploration of the vast area of the phenomenology of projective identification. Until Bion's theory of thinking and of groups slowly penetrated into actual clinical work around the early seventies, the preoccupation with projective identificatory phenomena, starting with my paper on anal masturbation, was certainly my own major research preoccupation. I mention that particular paper because it marks my awakening to the operation of projective processes not merely with external objects, but with internal ones as well. ·

It may be useful, at the outset, to indicate the scope of this small book. It is not a survey of the field of work in psychoanalysis which has centred on the concept of projective identification. It is, rather, an attempt to trace the influence of this concept in my own clinical work in the past fifteen years. Its emphasis, after a recapitulation of books and papers up to 1988 (*The Apprehension of Beauty* with Meg Harris Williams), will be on the outcome of investigations into the claustrophobic, the projective aspects of the twofold phenomenology of projective identification. By and large the contributions by most people to the evidences of the operation of this aspect of narcissism have been devoted to the identificatory phenomena, grandiosity, psychotic depressive states, hypochondria, confusional states. On the other hand explorations of the perversions and addictions have emphasized the aspect of narcissistic organization consequent to splitting processes. Similarly Bion's delineation of work group and basic assumption group was later amplified by his structural distinction between the adaptational carapace or exoskeleton of the personality, and its core or endoskeleton — the realm of emotional relationships where meaning is generated in psychic reality. But the interweaving of basic assumption group mentality and the structural basis of narcissistic organization was not spelled out until *A Memoir of the Future*. The elaboration of the concept of the Claustrum is also meant to give firmness to this connection.

The two steps in my own understanding of these matters which came as revelations, clinical discoveries, were the projective identification with internal objects consequent to masturbation with intrusive unconscious phantasies (1975), and the recognition of the compartmentalized aspects of the interior world of the internal maternal figure, first outlined in *Explorations in Autism* and later clarified in *Dream Life* (1984) and *Studies in Extended Metapsychology* (1986). I trust the utter egocentricity of the book will be forgiven. It is after all only a report of work-in-progress, already well known to the people with whom I work at home and abroad.

1   Melanie Klein's Vision of Projective Identification

Although her earlier work had borne the stamp of an emphasis on the concreteness of psychic reality and thus of internalized objects (the structural elements of the Superego), and established that the mechanisms of defense were implemented by unconscious phantasies, it was not until the 1946 paper on schizoid mechanisms, that Melanie Klein embarked on a path that clearly distinguished her work from Freud's, following a direction already indicated by Abraham's "Short Study of the Libido". While she never abandoned the distinction between Life and Death Instincts, her methods of description moved more and more away from differentiating between ego and id in clinical phenomena in favour of talking of the Self. This was ushered in by the description of splitting processes, in which parts of the self not only embraced Id aspects but also internal object aspects (*Narrative* Notes to the 24th Session).

The thrust of "Notes on some Schizoid Mechanisms" is, as its title suggests, towards defining mechanisms characteristic of the paranoid-schizoid position, therefore of the first part of the first year of post-natal life, and consequently the source of points of fixation, in her view, for the psychoses: that is schizophrenias, paranoia and manic-depressive states. "The persecutory fears arising from the infant's oral-sadistic impulses to rob the mother's body of its good contents, and from the anal-sadistic impulses to put his excrements into her (including the desire to enter her body in order to control her from within) are of great importance for the development of paranoia and schizophrenia." (p. 293, *Works* III).

It must be remembered that at that time she was viewing the earliest splitting processes as passive. "It seems to be in keeping with the lack of cohesiveness that under the pressure of this threat" (i.e. of anxiety of being destroyed from within) "the ego tends to fall to pieces" (p. 296). Active splitting was seen as probably a later development. Also of importance was her view that self and objects split, fall to pieces or are actively split, simultaneously. "I believe that the ego is incapable of splitting the object — internal and external — without a corresponding splitting taking place in the ego." (p. 298). She does not appear to consider the corresponding situation: can the ego split itself without splitting its objects? In her descriptions "ego" and "self" at first alternate, gradually yielding to a preference for "splitting of the self" when she comes to explain her view of the significance of these concepts for narcissism. "Insofar as the mother comes to contain bad parts of the self she is not felt to be a separate individual but is felt to be *the* bad self" (p. 300). This shift from a "Vicissitudes of Instincts" to a "Structural" view of narcissism, eventually called "Narcissistic Organization" by Rosenfeld, characterizes Melanie Klein's descriptions from this time on. This same narcissistic consequence was seen to result from splitting off and projecting good parts of the self "excessively": "— good parts of the personality are felt to be lost, and in this way the mother becomes the ego-ideal" (a distinction I cannot recall her later utilizing; perhaps she meant Freud's earlier use of ideal-ego). These were the first descriptions of a Narcissistic Identification. What was meant by a quantitative term such as "excessively" is puzzling. Elsewhere it seems mainly to mean aggressively, although not necessarily destructively. However the whole question of structure is a bit confused at this time by Mrs. Klein's embracing Paula Heimann's idea of the ego being "incapable of assimilating its internal objects".

Melanie Klein's vision of projective identification in "Notes" is very little clarified by the paper "On Identification" (1955) for even the implication that this phantasy operates exclusively with external objects is a bit equivocated by the uncertainty whether the events in the three days of Fabian's life prior to his death took place in the outside world or in a dream of his terminal delirium from heart disease. In fact very little more is said about this phenomenon (there is only one small mention in *Envy and Gratitude* 1957) until the notes on the *Narrative* (published after her death). Its clinical phenomenology is only hinted at; claustrophobia is only seen from the point of feeling imprisoned within the personality of the object of projective identification, while the relevance of schizoid mechanisms to the psychoses is described mainly from the points of view of integration-disintegration and regression to the paranoid-schizoid position.

8

Even the Notes to the *Narrative* give a poor yield with regard to the accruing of clinical meaning to this concept. Clearly by the late fifties when she was writing the *Narrative* her view of projective identification as a psychotic mechanism had altered:

> In the same hour Richard had expressed his greedily internalizing the mother, myself, in fact everybody, by the starfish-empire drawing. Now the red border represented the process of projective identification. The greedy part of himself — the starfish — had invaded the mother, and Richard's anxiety, feelings of guilt, and sympathy related to the mother's suffering both through his intrusion 'and through the bad father damaging and controlling her internally. In my view the processes of internalization and projective identification are complementary and operate from the beginning of post-natal life; they vitally determine object relations. The mother can be felt to be taken in with all her internalized objects; the subject, too, which has entered another person, may be felt to take with him his objects (and his relations with them). The further exploration of the vicissitudes of internalized object relations, which are at every step bound up with projective processes should, in my view, throw much light on the development of the personality and of object relations. (*Narrative*, p. 115, *Works* IV).

What is meant by "complementary" has some light thrown on it by a later note: "— a lessening of the violence of projective identification — implies a diminution in the strength of the paranoid and schizoid mechanisms and defenses and a greater capacity to work through the depressive position" (p. 250, Note to 51st session) and "This [i.e. drawing 49, the Empire eagle with its coat drawn over it showing only its face, which Richard demonstrated] is an instance of projective identification which is quickly followed, and possibly simultaneous with, internalization." (p. 279, Note to 56th session).

That projective identification and internalization are "complementary", one "quickly followed" by the other, perhaps even "simultaneously", seems to move relentlessly towards a recognition of the invasion of internal, that is already internalized, objects, but does not quite get there. It is further

9

hinted at when the process of projective identification is connected with masturbation: "— fears about the inside of his mother's body, in particular the fight with his father's penis inside the mother and in her vagina — relating to masturbation, had come up as a sequel to the analysis of intense internal persecution." (p. 165, note to 34th Session) Of course the analysis was done in 1940 and the clinical work does not reflect a fully formed concept of projective identification. Also, in the notes, Mrs. Klein is generally reluctant to re-formulate the material in keeping with later views. But it is clear that the manifestations of claustrophobic anxieties related to the playroom or when he comes for a few sessions to her lodgings, have not been seen as evidences of the operation of projective identification.

On the other hand the notes to the *Narrative* extend and clarify Mrs. Klein's views about the effect on the development of the personality and of object relations by the projective identification of good parts of the self:

'I would suggest that a securely established good object, implying a securely established love for it, gives the ego a feeling of riches and abundance which allows for an outpouring of libido and projection of good parts of the self into the external world without a sense of depletion arising. The ego can then also feel that it is able to re-introject the love it has given out, as well as take in goodness from other sources, and thus be enriched by the whole process' ("On Identification," p. 144, *Works* III).

This benign circle of projective identification and re-introjection would seem to be connected, in her view, with the combined part-object of breast and father's penis "losing in power" (note to 85th session) and a "greater belief in the goodness of the combined parents" (note to 91st session). It is not clear whether she felt that this improvement was brought about by withdrawal of projected bad parts, or by amelioration of envy by good experiences or by the clarified splitting and idealization of self and objects. The clinical work suggests all three.

Finally Mrs. Klein expresses some views about the ways in

which excessive splitting and projective identification leads to indiscriminate introjection and lack of integration in the self: "The indiscriminate introjection of various figures is in my view complementary to the strength of projective identification which leads to the feeling that parts of the self are distributed — a feeling which in turn reinforces such indiscriminate identifications." (Notes to 79th session.) The clinical material suggests that she has in view the processes of group participation and thus of adolescent phenomena.

In these notes to the *Narrative* Mrs. Klein is reluctant to link the theoretical findings with categories of psychopathology found in adult patients. There are indications, however, that she views projective identification as playing a role in male homosexuality, promiscuity and paranoid jealousy. Much was being contributed by other workers during her lifetime to the working out of the clinical implications of the operation of projective identification for depressive and manic states, hypochondria, confusional states and schizophrenic illnesses (Segal, Rosenfeld, Bion and others). Its role in communication processes became a central issue in the years following, particularly in the writings of Bion, Betty Joseph, Money-Kyrle and others. All these works rightly belong to the filling in of the Kleinian model of the mind. What follows in later chapters probably must be considered part of the Post-Kleinian model as it appears to go far beyond anything that Melanie Klein implied in her formulation and use of the concept of projective identification, and perhaps might also stand outside anything she would have agreed with.

2   Review of Earlier Publications

Since the aim of this book is both to bring together my earlier experience and ideas about projective identification, scattered in various publications, and to amend and amplify them with current views, all as a basis for exploring some of the wider social and political implications of this mental mechanism, I thought at first to republish here the earlier statements. But I find, on reviewing, that everything I have written in the past thirty years is shot through with reports of these phenomena. The only option is to take only the major publications in chronological order, abstracting from them the developing ideas.

But as an exception to this I have chosen to republish in full the paper "The Relation of Anal Masturbation to Projective Identification." It represents first of all a clinical discovery that surprised me, and secondly it is certainly the jumping off place for all subsequent developments in my thought on this subject. As a preamble I might mention that I had been very unhappy about Melanie Klein's paper "On Identification" but knew not why for some years. It seemed clear to me that, regardless of the author of the novel's wish to be ambiguous, there was no need for psycho-analytical ambiguity. Clearly, like Golding's '*Pincher Martin*', the story of Fabian represents the dream of a dying man. Its events therefore belong squarely in the inner and not the outer world. Only with the writing of this paper in 1966 did I discover the real reason for my dissatisfaction: the tendency of Mrs. Klein's paper to continue treating projective identification as a psychotic mechanism and one which operated with external objects, primarily or exclusively.

THE RELATION OF ANAL MASTURBATION TO PROJECTIVE IDENTIFICATION*

Introduction

When attempting to relate some character traits of the 'Wolf Man' to his intestinal symptoms, Freud (1918) was forced to the conclusion that an anal theory of femininity and an 'identification' with his mother's menorrhagia had antedated the patient's castration theory of femininity. Until Melanie Klein's establishment of the concept of 'projective identification' it was assumed that such a process would have been due solely to introjection. In her original description (1946, p.300) of projective identification, Klein linked it very closely to anal processes but nowhere else in her written work has this connexion been made more explicit.

Furthermore, the contribution made by anality to character formation, as studied by Freud (1908, 1917), Abraham (1921), Jones (1913, 1918), Heimann (1962), and others, has always been stated in terms of the outcome in character structure of the so-called 'sublimation' of anal fantasies, in which the emphasis has rested on the narcissistic over-evaluation of the faeces on the one hand and the object-relationship consequences of the toilet-training struggle on the other. The present paper intends to demonstrate the contribution to character formation made by the combination of all three factors working in complex relation to one another, namely narcissistic evaluation of the faeces, the confusions surrounding the anal zone (especially anus-vagina and penis-faeces confusions) and the identification aspect of anal habits and fantasies based on projective identification. In studying this problem in the analytic process, in close collaboration with several colleagues, I have been forced also to the recognition that masturbation of the anus is a far more wide-spread habit than the analytic literature to date would imply. Freud (1905, p.187; 1917, p.131) recognized its existence in children who employ both fingers and the faecal mass as the masturbatory object.

* Read at the 24th International Psycho-Analytical Congress, Amsterdam, July 1965. *Int.J. Psycho-Anal.* (1966) 47, pts.2-3.

However, Spitz's (1949) study of faecal play and his conclusions, based on observational and not analytic data, have promulgated an implication of severe pathology not substantiated by our own work.

For the sake of presentation, and partly to accord with the Congress theme of the Obsessional States, this paper is also focused on the character constellation of 'pseudo-maturity' which we find to be intimately related to anal erotism, a finding by no means at variance with the descriptions by Winnicott (1965) and by Deutsch (1942) of what they have called the 'false self' and the 'as if' personality type respectively. The relation of 'pseudo-maturity' to obsessional states will be demonstrated and shown to assume an oscillatory system at a certain stage of the analytic process, throwing some light on the background of obsessional character in a manner similar to the description of the cyclothymic background of obsessional neurosis given in my earlier (1963) paper. Clinical material and theoretical discussion will bind together the three concepts: anal masturbation, projective identification, pseudo-maturity.

The Characterology

Inadequate splitting-and-idealization (Klein, 1957), operative particularly after weaning, in relation to demands for cleanliness and aggravated by the expectation or arrival of younger siblings, contributes to a strong trend to idealize the rectum and its faecal contents. But this idealization is largely based on a confusion of identity due to the operation of projective identification, whereby the baby's bottom and that of the mother are confused one with the other, and both are equated with the mother's breasts.

As we reconstruct the scene from the analytic situation a typical sequence would appear as follows: after a feed, when placed in the cot, as mother walks away, the baby, hostilely equating mother's breasts with her buttocks, begins to explore its own bottom, idealizing its roundness and smoothness and eventually penetrating the anus to reach the retained, withheld faeces. In this process of penetration, a fantasy of secret intrusion into mother's anus (Abraham, 1921, p.389) to rob her takes shape, whereby the baby's

15

rectal contents become confused with mother's idealized faeces, felt to be withheld by her to feed daddy and the inside-babies.

The consequence of this is twofold, namely an idealization of the rectum as a source of food and the projective (delusional) identification with the internal mother which erases the differentiation between child and adult as regards capacities and prerogatives. The urine and flatus may also come in for their share of idealization.

In the excited and confused state which results from the anal masturbation, a bimanual masturbation of genital (phallus or clitoris) and anus (confused with vagina) tends to ensue, producing a sado-masochistic perverse coital fantasy in which the internal parental couple do great harm to one another. The projective identification with both internal figures which accompanies this bimanual masturbation harms the internal objects both by the violence of intrusion into them and by the sadistic nature of the intercourse it produces between them. Hypochondria as well as claustrophobic anxieties are thus an invariable consequence to some degree.

In childhood this situation encourages a pre-oedipal (ages 2 – 3) crystallization of character manifest by docility, helpfulness, preference for adult companionship, aloofness or bossiness with other children, intolerance of criticism, and high verbal capacity. When this characterological crust is broken momentarily by frustration or anxiety, outcrops of hair-raising virulence are laid bare — tantrums, faecal smearing, suicidal attempts, vicious assaults on other children, lying to strangers about parental maltreatment, cruelty to animals, etc.

This structure by-passes the Oedipus complex and seems to equip a child reasonably well superficially for academic and social life and may carry through into adulthood relatively unruffled even by the adolescent upheaval. But the 'pseudo' nature of the adjustment is apparent in adult life even where the perverse tendencies have not led to obviously aberrant sexual activities. The feeling of fraudulence as an adult person, the sexual impotence or pseudo-potency (excited by secret perverse fantasies), the inner loneliness and the basic confusion between good and bad, all create a life of tension and lack of satisfaction, bolstered, or rather compensated, only by the smugness and snobbery which are an inevitable accompaniment of massive projective identification.

Where this organization is less dominant and pervasive, or during analysis when it begins to give way to the therapeutic process, it stands in an oscillatory relation to an obsessional organization. There the internal objects are not penetrated, but are rather omnipotently controlled and separated on a less part-object level of relationship, as the focal difficulties have moved from separation anxieties toward the previously by-passed oedipal conflicts.

The delusional identification with the mother due to projective identification and the confusion between anus and vagina together produce rigidity and a sense of fraudulent femininity in women. In men these dynamics produce either homosexual activities or more frequently an intense dread of becoming homosexual (since the heightened femininity is not distinguished from passive anal homosexuality). Or conversely the secondary projective identification with the father's penis (in the ensuing bimanual masturbation) may produce a leading phallic quality in either male or female patients especially where omnipotent (manic) reparativeness has been mobilized as a defence against the severe underlying depression present in all such cases.

The Nature of the Transference

When this configuration of massive projective identification with the internal objects, usually on a part-object level as breast or penis, is active the cooperation of an adult sort in the analytic process is replaced by a psuedo-cooperation or 'helpfulness' to the analyst. This acting out shows itself in a somewhat slavish demeanour, a desire to convince, to demonstrate, to assist, or to relieve the analyst of his burdens. Material is therefore often of a predigested variety, sometimes given in 'headline' fashion or as superficial interpretations of mental states. All sense of the patient's wishing to elicit interpretation is absent, replaced by an evident desire for praise, approval, admiration, or even

17

gratitude from the analyst. When these are not forthcoming, the analyst's activities are often felt to evince lack of understanding, envious attacks on the patient's capacities, mere surliness, or frank sadism. This latter reception of interpretation can quickly lead to erotization and cause the interpretation to be experienced as a sexual assault.

Whether the patient is producing dreams, associations, or a factual account of his daily activities, the acting out aspect is so dominant that the interpretation of content is relatively useless unless coupled with a clear demonstration of the nature and basis of the behaviour. This of course results in sullenness of the nothing-I-ever-do-pleases-you variety. But by the painstaking demonstration of the acting out, by consistent elucidation of the cryptic masturbation, and finally through dream analysis, progress can usually be made.

Acting out of the infantile projective identification with internal figures is such a prominent part of the character that its continual demonstration as a contaminant in the patient's adult life must be undertaken. Even in the face of intense opposition this scrutiny must also include areas of the greatest pride, success, and apparent satisfaction such as work, 'creative' activities, relations to children, siblings, or continued solicitous helpfulness to aging parents. The significance of clothing for the women, cars for the men, and money-in-the-bank for all must be investigated, for they are sure to be found loaded with irrational significance. So skilled is the counterfeiting of maturity in thought, attitude, communication, and action that only the dreams make possible this teasing apart of infantile 'pseudo-mature' items from the adult pattern of life.

The Dreams

It is worth mentioning here that sensitivity to the anal masturbatory aspects of the adult patient's dreams is immeasurably increased by experience with child patients and psychotics. Much of what appears below derives its conviction from such sources:

(a) Idealization of the faeces as food — dreams of scavenging and finding are in this category: finding apples among the autumn leaves, food in the empty larder, reaching into places the inside of which cannot be visualized, or underneath structures. Fishing and hunting may also come into this category, though not generally; but gardening, shopping, and stealing of food do, especially if the place is represented as dark, dirty, cheap or foreign.

(b) Idealization of the rectum — dreams in which the rectum is represented as a retreat or refuge generally show it as an eating place (restaurant or café, kitchen or dining room) but with qualities which announce its significance. It may be dirty, dark, smelly, cheap, crowded, smoky, below ground level, noisy, run by foreigners, in a foreign city. The food may be unappetizing, unhygienic, unhealthy, fattening, over-cooked, homogeneous (custards, puddings, etc), or catering to infantile greed in quantity or sweetness. Where rectum and breast are confused such configurations as outdoor cafés or market places with the above characteristics may appear.

(c) Idealization of the toilet situation (Abraham, 1920, p.318) — this often appears in dreams as sitting in lofty or exciting places, often looking down at water (lakes, canyons, streams) or sitting in places where food is being prepared, or in a position of importance ('Last Supper' dreams) or where people behind the dreamer are waiting for food, payment, services, or information (conducting an orchestra, serving at an altar).

(d) Representation of the anally masturbating fingers — these appear in dreams represented as parts of the body, people, animals, tools or machines, either singly or in groups of four or five, with qualities of faecal contamination variously represented or denied, such as negroes, men in brown helmets, soiled or shiny garden tools, white gloves, people dressed in black, earth-moving tractors, dirty children, worms, rusty nails, etc.

(e) Dreams showing the process of intrusion into the anus of the object (Abraham, 1921, p.389) — most frequently seen as entering a building or a vehicle, either furtively, by a back entrance, the door has wet paint, the entrance is very narrow, protective clothing must be worn, it is underground, under water, in a foreign country or closed to the public, etc.

(f) Idealization of the rectum as a source of pseudo-analysis

— this is frequent and may appear as secondhand bookshops, piles of old newspapers, filing cabinets, public libraries — one patient before an examination dreamed that he fished in the Fleet Street sewer and caught an encyclopaedia.

Clinical Material

I have chosen the following material to show the complexity of the connexions to orality and genitality which infuse the anal masturbatory situation and its attendant projective identification with such defensive power.

Three years of analytic work with a late adolescent young man had begun to press toward the dependent relationship to the breast which his history suggested would be extremely disturbed, for he had been a poor feeder, a complaining baby, and a tyrannical child in his dependence on his mother. We knew something of his capacity for scathing mockery and of a terrible way of laughing contemptuously, but this had seldom been unleashed in the consulting room, where his behaviour tended to be superficially cooperative, 'churning out fantasies', as he called it, all with an air of insincerity which made even the simplest account of a daily happening sound like confabulation. This we had already understood as 'pretending to be insincere' but indistinguishable to himself from 'pretending to pretend to be insincere', all of which related to a deeply-fixed paranoid feeling of being overheard by a hidden persecutor.

He dreamed that he was among friends and seemed once again, as in school days, to be the head boy. As they came over the *brow* of a hill, he saw a man, whom he knew to be a murderer, among some gravestones, just wandering about. Reassuring his friends that he knew how to handle the man, he approached him with an aide and, pretending to be friendly, led him down to the *bottom*, hoping to extract a confession.

ASSOCIATIONS — his tongue seems to be exploring the back of his teeth which feel old and cracked. That makes him think of putting on some slippers like the ones his father used to have. INTERPRETATION — that his teeth are represented by the gravestones and his tongue as the murderer among his victims. His device in the dream is to rid his mouth of these dangerous qualities and transform them into slippery fingers which can be led down to his bottom, where the victims can be identified in his faeces. But by this device his finger-in-his-bottom becomes confused with father's penis-in-mother's-vagina, an important source of the Nazi-daddy-who-kills-mummy's-Jewish-babies whom we know so well from earlier work. ASSOCIATIONS — he feels as if a circular saw were cutting his thigh (reference to surgery for hernia in puberty). He imagines himself with his back to double doors and the analyst outside trying to pull them open (projection of the buttock-spreading onto the analyst-surgeon-daddy). ASSOCIATION — an ornately-carved gilt picture frame (the analyst's interpretation is an ornate picture intended to frame him by revealing his guilt), the Mafia — the black hand. A boat going through a canal which is shaped to fit its keelless hull (the Mafia-fascist daddy getting the big black penis-finger into his anal canal, reassuring him in an Italian accent: 'No keel!')

These associations are typical of the punning which characterizes the compulsive anal masturbatory fantasies.

Four weeks later, approaching the Christmas holiday, in a state of mounting resentment and increasing difficulty at work due to acting out, he came fifteen minutes late and tracked mud from an unpaved road (a shortcut from the underground station to the consulting room) into my room. Only once before had he done this.

ASSOCIATIONS — he had rubbishy dreams over the week-end and feels reluctant to impose them on the analyst. INTERPRETATION — this conscious wish to spare is contrasted by an unconscious wish to dirty the analyst inside and out with his faeces, a bit of which has been acted out by tracking the dirt into the room. Patient looked with surprise at the floor, and apologised. ASSOCIATIONS — On Saturday night he dreamed he was tossing and turning in pain due to a dislocated finger (shows uninjured left index finger). INTERPRETATION — link with the gravestone dream. The week-end distress felt as due to the removal of his murderer-finger (Mafia) from its accustomed location. ASSOCIATIONS — but then he seemed at school, idle and bored. He wandered into the men's lavatory, where there seemed to be a nice big clean bathtub. He decided to have a bath, but then it changed to a small, filthy

21

station toilet with pornographic writing and pictures on the wall, just opposite the basement of a big department store. He couldn't decide what to do, because the staff of the store kept watching him suspiciously. He kept going in and out of the lavatory, until finally he entered the store to steal something.

This dream shows with unusual clarity the way in which the current separation situation (the dislocated finger at the boring week-end) leads to a sequence of infantile events, first wetting himself (the bath) with warm urine, then exploring his anus (the filthy toilet), becoming more and more sexually aroused (the pornography) and preoccupied with projective identification fantasies about the bottom of mother's body (the toilet-rectum across from the department-store-vagina with the watchful staff-penis) and his wish to rob her.

Sunday night's dream, approaching with some anxiety the Monday session, reveals the continuation of the infantile state, now a baby with soiled nappy, bottom, and cot. In the dream he wanted to change his clothes for a party he and friends were giving at his flat, but already every room was filled with guests, laughing, drinking and smoking (his soiled cot and nappy). But then he was in the park and felt happy among the greenery, even though he had on nothing but an undershirt (the baby has kicked off its nappy and idealizes its soiled bottom and cot). He finds a football to kick and soon others have joined him in the game (playing with his faeces).

This latter state, self-idealization through athletics, had appeared literally in hundreds of dreams in the first two years of his analysis. Here we see in detail its derivation. It is worth mentioning that this patient had suffered from a chronic, but non-ulcerative diarrhoea since early childhood which had only abated some eight months earlier in the analysis.

The Cryptic Anal Masturbation

Reconstruction from the transference indicates that anal masturbation becomes cryptic very early in childhood and tends to remain both unnoticed and unrecognized in its significance thereafter, except when frank perversions declare themselves in adolescence or later. I have referred to it as 'cryptic' to emphasise here the unconscious skill with which it is hidden from scrutiny.

The most common form (see Freud, and Abraham) utilizes the faecal mass itself as the masturbatory stimulant. Either its retention, slow expulsion, rhythmic partial expulsion and retraction, or the rapid, forced, and painful expulsion are accompanied by the unconscious fantasies which alter the ego state. This change in mental state can be noted in child patients when they return from defaecating during sessions. The habit of reading on the toilet, special methods of cleansing the anus, special concern about leaving a bad smell, anxiety about faecal stain on underclothing, habitually dirty finger nails, surreptitious smelling of fingers, etc. all are tentative indicators of cryptic anal masturbation. But it can skilfully be hidden far afield from the act of defaecation: in bathing habits, the wearing of constrictive undergarments, in cycling, horseback riding or other activities which stimulate the buttocks. Most difficult perhaps of all to locate is the sequestration of anal masturbation in the genital sexual relation, which is invariably the case to some extent while anus and vagina are still confused with one another. On the other hand, like Poe's 'Purloined Letter', it may be flamboyantly in view, as in constipation with enemata, suppositories for recurrent fissure *in ano*, etc. but its significance denied.

While it is not part of my technique to comment on a patient's behaviour on the couch nor to ask for associations to it, scrutiny of the patterns of posture and movement and linking them with dream material does sometimes permit a fruitful interpretation of the behaviour. By this means the series of modifications of the anal masturbation can be revealed and a more successful search for the actual anal stimulation instituted. For instance, a patient who often kept both hands in his pockets recognized through a dream that this was accompanied at times by pulling at a loose thread. This led to the realization that he had a habit of manually teasing apart peri-anal hairs prior to defaecation lest they spoil the shape of his emerging faecal mass.

The Analytic Process

The early years of analysis in such cases involve primarily the resolution of the self-idealization and spurious

23

independence, through the establishment of the capacity in the transference to utilize the analytic breast for projective relief (the toilet-breast). The relief of confusional states (Klein, 1957) takes the forefront, especially those confusions of identity and therefore about time and the adult-child differential which characterize massive projective indentification. It is only after several years, when the attachment to the feeding breast is developing and the intolerance to separations is rhythmically being invoked at week-ends and holidays, that these processes can be accurately and fruitfully investigated. It seems certain that, unless the cryptic anal masturbation can be discovered and its insidious production of aberrant ego states scotched at source, further progress is seriously impeded.

This brings us to a most important point in our exposition, for I would suggest from my experience that the dynamic here described is often of such a subtle structure, the pressure on the analyst to join in the idealization of the pseudo-maturity so great, and the underlying threats of psychosis and suicide so covertly communicated that many of the 'successful' analyses which break down months or years after termination may fall into this category. It is necessary therefore also to stress that the countertransference position is extremely difficult and in every way repeats the dilemma of the parents, who found themselves with a 'model' child, so long as they abstained from being distinctly parental, either in the form of authority, teaching, or opposition to the relatively modest claims for privileges beyond those to which the child's age and accomplishments could reasonably entitle it.

The seductiveness must not be thought of as mere hypocrisy nor its loving quality a sham. Far from it, a Cordelia-like tenderness can be quite genuine, but the preconditions for loving are incompatible with growth since they are both intensely possessive and subtly denigrating of their objects. Termination of analysis is quietly pursued as a fiat for a non-analytic and interminable relation to the analyst and to psycho-analysis. Needless to say, therefore, the configuration described in this paper is of special interest and concern for the analyst with patients who have a professional or social link with psycho-analysis.

In my experience, where the seduction of the analyst to idealize the achievement of pseudo-maturity, in its newly modified and 'analysed' edition, is firmly resisted, interruption of the analysis may be forced by the patient for ostensibly 'realistic' reasons. This may be done through engineering a geographical shift, a change in marital status, by promoting opposition from parent or marital partner, by contracting financial obligations which render payment for the analysis infeasible, etc., while still clinging to the idealized positive transference. If the analytic penetration is to succeed, a prolonged period of violently negative transference and manifest uncooperativeness must be expected and may prove intractable. This takes the form of injured innocence, self-pity, and the constant complaint that the analyst's implication that anal masturbation exists and continues in fact is either doctrinaire, a projection, or a manifestation of outside interference (e.g., from a supervisor).

Thanks to the constant clarification brought by dreams it is usually possible for the analyst to persevere. Gradually, by urging improved cooperation about consciously withheld associations and closer attention to body habits, the analyst can bring the hidden anal masturbation to light. With this the feeding-breast transference breaks through the restrictions imposed upon it by the idealization-of-the-faeces. Full-blown, painful and analytically fruitful experiences of separation anxiety become possible for the first time.

It is at this point in the analytic process that the relation to obsessional characterology becomes evident. The oscillation of the two states, pseudo-maturity and obsessional states, can be seen to take place, as the Oedipus complex in its genital and pregenital aspects takes the forefront of the transference. It can be understood that, for all the oedipal implications of earlier material which had required interpretation, a full experience of oedipal conflict only becomes possible when the differentiation of adult and infantile parts of the self has been thus arduously established.

Further Clinical Material

The clinical material which follows is intended to demonstrate the way in which strengthening of the alliance to good

25

objects internally and to the analyst in the transference make possible a new stand against old anal habits. The patient in question came to analysis because of lack of direction in his work but analysis soon revealed also the pseudo-mature structure outlined in the paper. It also brought to light a little noticed continuation of anal habits and preoccupations which could be traced back in the anamnesis to nocturnal games with an older brother, probably never overtly sexual. But the unconscious splitting-off and projecting of a bad part of the self into the brother had played a large part in the self-idealization which underlay the patient's 'goodness' as a child. In fact the brother was by no means a bad child nor a bad sibling.

Approaching a Christmas holiday, the patient's recurrent fissure *in ano* became active again as the material swung toward patterns of anal intrusion into internal objects already well known by this fourth year of the analysis.

On a Tuesday, he reported having felt ill and cold since the unsatisfactory session of the day before. He dreamed that he was in a house with a man his younger brother's age and yet it was also the patient himself as a younger man. This fellow seemed friendly and pleasant at first and was telling the patient that the bodies of police inspectors, often in a state of advanced decomposition, were being found all over Britain. Only when he indicated that there was one such in the next room under a sheet did the patient become alarmed. When the young man invited him to see it and the patient demurred, a tense situation arose. The patient backed toward the door and finally dashed out as the young man lunged for his throat. To his surprise there were policemen outside who reassured him that road blocks were already established and the young murderer would be dealt with.

In the second dream of the same night he found himself walking on the pavement, naked but for a tiny bath-towel, acutely embarrassed that his penis was visible. Thinking to get home more quickly and cut short the distress, he headed for a station, but was intercepted by a tramp who invited him to his nearby lodgings. He gladly accepted, but once in the tramp's bed he could not get to sleep, for the tramp stood upright by the bed all night and frightened him.

Note the contrast in these two dreams. In the first he is able to resist involvement in anal sadistic oedipal attacks on police-inspector daddies and finds himself comforted by the external relation to the analyst and analytic road-block process. But in the second dream oedipal humiliation in the bath-analysis drives him back to the anal preoccupation with a bad tramp-brother's faecal-penis in his rectum (the constipation which is a regular prelude to activity of his anal fissure).

On the Friday he complained of his constipation and noted that he had begun to diet in an obsessional way. An amusing incident had occurred the previous evening in which a 'fat' fly was buzzing about the house, finally landing on a vase. As he announced his intention to 'show the old gentleman to the door', picking up the vase with the sluggish fly on it, his young son wittily took the patient's arm and led *him* toward the door. He dreamed that he was waiting for a haircut in a queue, but it took so long, despite the fact that both man and wife were barbering on two chairs, that he despaired. Then he found himself lying comfortably in a little flat-bottomed boat going through a little tunnel (like one he'd been on as a child on a visit to Father Christmas at a big department store). When the boat was meant to make a right angled turn to the left, it became stuck, so the patient put his right hand into the water, making a scooping motion (as he had done the night before when the kitchen sink drain was blocked, to clear it). But he realized with a shock that his fingers were in the mouth of a tramp, lying in the water beneath the boat, who was about to bite him (anxiety about the constipation leading to the tearing open of his fissure, in contrast to the gentle 'showing-the-fat-old-gentleman-(fly)-to-the-door').

In his dream confirmation of the intolerance of separation (the couch-boat turning to the left; in fact when the patient leaves the couch it is *he* who makes a right-angled turn to the right) and turning to the tramp-faeces brother inside the mother's Father-Christmas-tunnel, is impressive. Note how the wish to rid himself gently of his oedipal rival (as his son's joke makes clear) leads him again to the alliance with the tramp brother, the constipated faecal penis and the tearing-open-the-fissure type of anal masturbatory defaecation. The infantile wish to make daddy old and expel him anally is still overpoweringly active, even though the patient's struggle

27

against an abandonment to anal sadism has well commenced.

Three weeks later, on a Monday, he reported himself in a peculiar mood, full of intense and mixed feelings toward the analysis, aware that a recent insight helped him to curb a frequent type of provocative behaviour toward his wife but very worried and resentful about the coming holiday break. He dreamed that he was at a pond near my consulting room, waiting to go to his session. A man was fishing, though there are no fish in that pond, and had one of his two hooks stuck in the bottom. The patient had to free it, but was afraid the man would cruelly keep the line tight and cause the patient to be hooked. In fact this is exactly what happened. Determined to be free, he tore the hook out of his finger with pliers, tearing a piece of the flesh with it. To have it dressed he needed to go to a town outside London to see the American Ambassador. He was being fêted in a horsedrawn carriage before returning to the States; but, nonetheless, left the carriage and dressed the patient's finger and took him to his home. There the patient, feeling very happy, watched the Ambassador and his family have their lunch, separated from him by a perforated partition.

Here, before a holiday, the struggle to accept the oedipal distress (wound on his finger, linked to circumcision), and to free himself from the addiction to the anal masturbation (the man with his hook caught in the bottom on the pond, linked to the tramp-brother faecal penis) has proceeded with remarkable rapidity and clarity of insight. It is interesting that subsequently on two occassions he developed a paronychia of an index finger at week-ends.

SUMMARY

For the purpose of illustrating a current trend of our researches into the intimate connexion between projective identification and anal masturbation, I have chosen to describe the transference manifestations of a type of character disorder seen with relative frequency among the many intelligent, gifted and outwardly successful people who seek analysis, namely of 'pseudo-maturity'. The concept of projective identification, first described by Melanie Klein, has opened the way to a new fruitful investigation of hitherto unexplored aspects of anality. By demonstrating how projective identification with internal objects is induced by anal masturbation, a richer conception of the derivation and significance of the narcissistic evaluation of faeces is unfolded, thus linking the anal phase more surely to symptom and character pathology.

REFERENCES

ABRAHAM, K. (1920). 'The narcissistic evaluation of excretory processes in dreams and neurosis.' In: *Selected Papers* (London: Hogarth, 1927.)
— (1921). 'Contributions to the theory of the anal character.' *ibid.*
DEUTSCH, H. (1942). 'Some forms of emotional disturbance and their relationship to schizophrenia.' *Psychoanal. Quart.,* **11.**
FREUD, S. (1905). *Three Essays on the Theory of Sexuality, S.E.,* **7.**
— (1908). 'Character and anal erotism.' *S.E.,* **9.**
— (1917). 'On transformations of instinct as exemplified in anal erotism.' *S.E.,* **17.**
— (1918). 'From the history of an infantile neurosis.' *S.E.,* **17.**
HEIMANN, P. (1962). 'Notes on the anal stage.' *Int. J. Psycho-Anal.,* **43.**
JONES, E. (1913). 'Hate and anal erotism in the obsessional neurosis.' In: *Papers on Psycho-Analysis,* 2nd and subsq. editions. (London: Baillière, 1918).
— (1918). 'Anal-erotic character traits.' *ibid.*
KLEIN, M. (1946). 'Notes on some schizoid mechanisms.' In: *Developments in Psycho-Analysis* ed. Klein *et al.* (London: Hogarth, 1952).
— (1957). *Envy and Gratitude* (London: Tavistock.)
MELTZER, D. (1963). 'A contribution to the metapsychology of cyclothymic states.' *Int. J. Psycho-Anal.,* **44.**
SPITZ, R. (1949). 'Autoerotism.' *Psychoanal. Study Child,* **3 – 4.**
WINNICOTT, D. W. (1965). *The Maturational Processes and the Facilitating Environment* (London: Hogarth.)

I have often thought this was the best and most interesting paper I have ever written. I had studied pseudo-maturity in children during my years as a child psychiatrist in the U.S. during my Freudian training but without picking up anything of the present constellation. My interest now was chiefly focussed on the evidence of projective identification with internal objects, although as yet I had little suspicion of the scope of such operations. As with Mrs. Klein's description, it was the identificatory aspect, delusional and manic in quality, that I discerned. While the clinical material revealed qualities of the space, mummy's rectum, I did not yet see it as a life-space. Therefore I did not really pick up the claustrophobic implications in the material.

The paper does not sufficiently deal with the aspect of omnipotence with which the intrusion phantasy is carried out, and therefore does not emphasise the importance of the masturbatory act itself and the excitement it generates. Perhaps Mrs. Klein's emphasis on the importance of the unconscious rather than the conscious phantasies accompanying masturbation drew attention away from the importance of the excitement and orgasm. It has long been my contention that the significance of the act of masturbation is quite a separate issue from that of the phantasies, conscious or unconscious. Work with psychotic adults and children has convinced me that the act of masturbation, of whatever orifice or body part, derives its urgency and often compulsive force from its capacity to generate omnipotence. This issue was taken up in the following year in the Appendix to *The Psycho-analytical Process*.

I will now turn my attention to that book, first published by Heinemann and reprinted by our Clunie Press. Although the *Explorations in Autism*, written with John Bremner, Shirley Hoxter, Doreen Weddell and Isca Wittenberg was not published until eight years later in 1975, the work behind both books was going on at the same time. They both grew out of my connection with the Child Psycho-therapy Training at the Tavistock Clinic, directed first by Esther Bick and later by Martha Harris. A rich experience of supervision of work with children and a great freedom to lecture on whatever interested me proved a forcing house to my ideas, promoting probably the richest period of my analytic life. Bion's ideas were taking stronger hold in my work with adult patients but undoubtedly the phenomenology of projective identification held the dominant position in my interests, with children in particular. The events of the playroom make the infantile phantasies so concrete. Let me quote Shirley Hoxter's elegant description of Piffie's way of entering the playroom:

The very literal way he experiences putting himself into my body was shown by the routines he developed for entering the house and making his way to my upstairs consulting room. On entering the house he would make a plunging dive onto the floor. He would then crawl slowly and painfully upstairs pushing his head against each step and saying, 'Come and help me push these plop-plop steps away.' Or frequently he would take out a stair-rod and beat each step, saying: 'Baby, baby', or hold the stick in front of his penis and use it to thrust his way into the room. Just before entering the room he sometimes knelt and spun around as if he were a drill, saying, 'Mummy-hole' and then twiddle his hands round and round, saying, 'Wee-wee hole'. (p.168)

Comparable phenomenology enacted in the transference by adult patients, as indicated in the "Anal Masturbation" paper, are pale in comparison and may be difficult to recognize for analysts who have not worked with children, whence conviction about the concreteness of these activities for psychic reality derives.

The upshot of this cumulative experience with children, which sprung fully armed, to my astonishment, in extemporaneous lectures in Buenos Aires was the description of the "Sorting of Geographical Confusions" in *The Psycho-analytical Process*. Since it is short and condensed, I will reproduce it here in full and then discuss it.

THE SORTING OF GEOGRAPHICAL CONFUSIONS

In the first Chapter I have described my experience of the initial phase of the analytic process with children, carrying as a central thesis the contention that this process has a natural history of its own, determined by the structure of the mental apparatus at deeply unconscious levels. If this process is adequately presided over by the analyst through the creation of an adequate setting and through an interpretive intervention sufficiently correct and timely to modify the severest anxieties and facilitate working-through, a sequence of phases can be seen (in retrospect mainly) to have emerged, the second of which I wish now to illustrate.

The first week-end separation sets in train a modality of relationship at deep levels of the unconscious which is increased in intensity as the infantile transference processes are gathered and brought to bear in the analysis. This modality, or the trend toward it, is released by every regular separation experience and, later in analysis, will be revived by every *un*planned break in the analytic continuity. The modality to which I refer is the infantile tendency to massive projective identification with external, and soon also with internal, objects. It arises from a configuration of motives and gives rise to a spectrum of consequences which need detailed examination. First, however, a general economic' principle should be clarified. The duration of the phase dominated by any particular transference organisation is not really predictable at present, as the factors governing mobility of defences, the intensity of the drive toward integration, the capacity to accept dependence, etc., are all at present obscure and are ordinarily put together under the rubric of "constitutional", which, whatever its biological reference, in practice probably means that we can only assess them in retrospect but not in prospect. In the second place, the term "dominate the transference" must also be taken as a relative one, since the economics of that disposition is obscure. The analytic process is a cyclical one, and the phases which I trace here in a panoramic way can to some degree be seen to appear in sequence in every session, every week, every term, every year — that is, in all four of the cyclical time units of the analytic process. The phase under discussion, being concerned with the experience of separation and of separate identity, naturally tends more to dominate the beginning and end of such cycles — session, week, term, year. But one can reasonably say that the analysis itself is being "dominated" by this dynamism as long as it occupies an overwhelming portion of the analytic time and until the anxieties with which it is concerned have been elucidated so that the working-through can commence. It is probably a correct view that this working-through never completely ceases, which is only another way of saying that the struggle against regression and disintegration is continual.

Turning now to the various motives underlying the

tendency to massive projective identification, the major ones could be briefly listed as follows: intolerance of separation; omnipotent control; envy; jealousy; deficiency of trust; excessive persecutory anxiety. These can immediately be seen to overlap — or rather to interlock.

(1) Intolerance to separation can be said to exist when there is present an absolute dependence on an external object in order to maintain integration. This can be seen in autistic and schizophrenic children in whom the need for physical contact, or constant attention, or to be held in contact by constant verbalisation, reveals the absence of the psychic equivalent of the skin. They require an external object to hold together the parts of the self so as to form an area of life space inside the self which can contain the objects of psychic reality.

(2) Where the differentiation between good and bad is poorly defined due to inadequate or faulty splitting-and-idealization of self and objects, the use of projective identification for the purposes of omnipotent control can be seen to operate as a precondition for an object relation, in preference to narcissistic organisation. This is evident in very paranoid structure (*see* Betty Joseph's paper "Persecutory Anxiety in a four year old Boy", *Int. J. Psycho-Anal.,* Vol. XLVII).

(3) The role of envy we need not devote much time to as it has been so richly explored by Melanie Klein in *Envy and Gratitude* and *On Identification*.

(4) Jealousy is a complicated emotion and its differentiation from envy can often be somewhat more complicated than the 2-body or 3-body formulation suggested by Melanie Klein. This difficulty comes from two directions: there is a primitive elaboration of envy of the mother or the father or of their coital relationship which is so oral, so part-object and so sanctimonious in its application that I have called it "delusional jealousy" (even though this comes dangerously close to the term "delusions of jealousy" used in the psychiatric literature on paranoia, etc.). This jealousy is delusional because it is based on an *omniscient* relation to the mother's body which envisages internal babies disporting themselves in every conceivable way, especially those ways most longed for and frustrated in the infantile organisation. It

is not actually jealousy because it is in fact a devious representation of an envious attitude toward the adult figures.

In the second place there is possessive-jealousy which would appear to be a primitive, highly oral and part-object form of love. It is 2-body and yet is not really envy; it might seem to be included in Melanie Klein's description of envy-of-the-breast-that-feeds-itself. It is seen with extraordinary intensity in the autistic children and in children whose drive to maturity is very low, so that they wish either to remain infantile or to die. This means in their unconscious to return-to-sleep-inside-mother. It is this primitive form of possessive jealousy which plays an important role in perpetuating massive projective identification of this peculiar withdrawn, sleepy sort.

(5) Deficiency of trust is more doubtful as a factor at this phase, since it is generally a consequence of excessively destructive projection. But I think it can be isolated in a particular form related to secretiveness or trickiness. Where the mode of entry in projective identification is accomplished, in phantasy, by a deception or ruse, rather than by violence, distrust of the object, and consequent claustrophobia is intense, since the object is suspected of super-trickiness in its apparent vulnerability. This seems to me to be a distinctive phenomenon which cannot be attributed to parental inconsistency or deception since it appears in analysis as a positive preference for a cloak-and-dagger world. It plays an important role in paranoia and in the perverse attitude generally.

(6) Finally we come to the factor of excessive persecutory anxiety. Here I would think we are now in a position to make a qualitative distinction to enlarge on the general quantitative principle laid down by Melanie Klein, with special reference to what W. R. Bion has called "nameless dread"* and I have described as "terror". In both cases, paranoid anxieties which are fundamentally unbearable in quality have been described, as distinguished from other forms of persecution which may rise to an intensity which is unbearable in quantity.

Before outlining the consequences of this massive attack on the individuality of objects, and of the analyst in the transference, it is useful to attempt to catalogue briefly some of the

---

* *Learning From Experience* — (Heinemann) 1962

typical behavioural manifestations seen in the playroom. A tenable classification might be as follows: (*a*) utilization of the body of the analyst as a part of the self; (*b*) utilization of the room as the inside of an object; in such situations the analyst tends to represent a part-object inside this object, while being also equated with the object; (*c*) reversal of the adult-child relationship; where the analyst is made to contain and represent an alienated part of the infantile self; (*d*) exertion of omnipotent control over the analyst.

(*a*) It is more characteristic of younger children and of autistic and very psychotic children to make a frontal approach to the body of the analyst. Here technique plays a large part in determining either its perseverance or its mutation into forms employing somewhat more symbol formation. Probably the autistic children are the most persistent in this matter, despite technical attempts to divert it, and a case may perhaps be made for its toleration temporarily if the child is clearly driven by anxiety about fragmentation. Climbing on the lap, looking into eyes, ears and mouth, concrete representations of eating the analyst's words, pushing the head into the analyst's abdomen, encircling the body by the analyst's arms, pushing the genital or bottom against the analyst — these are some typical modes of approach. When yielded to, an almost immediate manic sweep follows and a shift of material can be seen. An autistic boy will rush to the window and gesture in triumph toward the birds in the garden, though they are usually the objects of enraged fist-shaking when he feels that he is outside and the garden is experienced as the inside of the mother's body. After hearing a dog bark in the garden, a little boy leaned against me briefly, then made a dive behind the couch and barked excitedly.

These types of contact may result in a state of massive projective identification, the physical contact providing an experience of a portal of entry. I mention this at some length to distinguish it as a general problem connected with projective identification, from attitudes and behaviour toward the analyst's body which are *manifestations of an existing state* of projective identification. An autistic child in such an existing state will take the analyst's hand to use it as a tool to open a door or cut a piece of paper. A paranoid child may scheme to get or demand to wear the analyst's glasses in order to see more clearly or try to use his pen, convinced that he could write or draw if he had it.

(*b*) Utilization of the room as the inside of an object is often made clear by the very mode of entry into the room, in a rush, or knocking against the door jamb, or by a mode of looking about as if in a vast arena. Conversely the phantasy of having remained sequestered inside the analyst during a separation may be expressed by hiding behind the door in the waiting room or under a chair. Looking out of the window, even on to a bare brick wall, as in my own playroom, can become a significant mode of activity, and throwing objects out of the door or window may figure as a way of representing the expulsion of rivals or persecutors. Confusion about time can often be noted as an accompanying phenomenon so that claustrophobic anxiety may be expressed by a suspicious monitoring of the analyst's watch. The intense erotization of the situation is often manifest and may express itself by complaints about the room being hot or by intense sensitivity to, and curiosity about, sounds from other areas of the house. The walls of the room often seem highly erotized, are felt and stroked, or conversely may be objects of sadistic inquiry by burrowing, investigating the entry and exit of pipes, wires, the structure of doors and windows and the origins of structural or decorative defects.

The relation to the analyst at such times is peculiar and mixed. Less psychotic children will maintain a running commentary with the analyst, while dramatising their phantasies of entry, possession, entrapment, persecution, etc. More psychotic or younger children are more likely to become lost in the phantasy and ignore the analyst as a person, so that the analyst feels, in his interpretive work, as if he were an outside observer and commentator. At other times he may figure as a part-object-inside-the-mother, usually the father's penis or an inside-baby, in either case persecutory, even if highly erotic in significance. It is at such times, in my experience, that the most unexpected explosions of anxiety may occur and, in keeping with this, outbreaks of unusually dangerous aggression. For some reason, probably connected with the phantasy of intrusion and the fear of being spied out, the analyst's eyes seem to be a particular object of attack. But even more dangerous is the sudden identification with the persecutor which may terminate anxiety attacks, resulting in vicious and uncompromising assault.

(c) Reversal of the adult-child relation may be the most prominent representation of massive projective identification and must, like the exerting of omnipotent control, be carefully distinguished from role-playing as a mode of communication. It is seen particularly in children starting school, in school-phobies, or their converse, in the child who assaults other children at school. I find that children who have split-off and projected valuable and constructive parts of the self ("mutilations of the ego") and are functioning at a defective level with much despair about maturation and learning — that these children also become tyrannical teachers or irritable mothers for very long and discouraging periods of analysis. The analyst in such cases is not really requested to act a role but is treated *as* a child, often one among many imaginary children in the playroom.

(d) This process of reversal shades subtly into the process of exerting omnipotent control over the analyst. Every conceivable technique is involved, verbal and non-verbal, ranging from coercion, threats, seduction, blackmail, pretended helplessness, feigned crying, exacting promises — all of which can be summed up by one concept, an attempt to induce the analyst to commit a breach of technique. The fact that the omnipotent control is exerted through the phantasy of projective identification is not immediately evident but is seen in the consequences of a breach of technique forced by one of the above methods. The material may suddenly shift to inside-the-object modes already mentioned with evident claustrophobic anxieties. Or an immediate manic response with delayed hypochondriacal consequences may be the result. In a more psychotic patient an immediate shift of most striking type can take place with analyst-like behaviour, making interpretations, commencing a lecture or scolding of a contemptuous sort. On the other hand a sudden regression may be seen, with infantile posturing, finger sucking, going to

37

sleep. Most confounding perhaps is an acute anxiety attack with rushing from the room and refusal to return, in which case prompt recognition and interpretation of the technical breach and of the concrete experience of omnipotent entry and control are required.

It must be understood that the term "breach of technique" is one which refers to the particular analyst's established modes for managing the setting. Early in analysis, when activities requiring technical handling are likely to be at their height, these modes have seldom been elaborated in detail. Certainly I for one am in favour of a gradual working out of such modes with each individual child, starting with a rather loose technique which can be tightened as indicated by events particularly of the types described under headings (a) and (d) ("utilization of the analyst's body" and "exerting of omnipotent control"). By this means, imposing restrictions on the basis of clear instances of untoward consequences in the analysis, frees the process from qualities of rigidity which always appear as arbitrary and basically hostile in the child's eyes.

Having now to some extent explored the motives for the massive projective identification which blurs the boundaries of self and object in the transference and produces attendant geographical confusion, and having described some of the typical forms of behaviour by which it is manifest in the analytic session, we are free to turn to a more general consideration of the analytic process as a whole and the role played in it by this phase. I have tried in the earlier sections to make clear that the basic problem is one of psychic pain and the need for an object in the outside world that can contain the projection of it — in a word, what I have come to call the "toilet-breast". By this name I mean to convey both the part-object nature of the relationship and the quality of being valued and needed, but not loved. This I think is very important to recognise in order to understand the inevitable dearth of depressive anxieties in this phase. That is not to say that depressive anxieties are not emerging during this period of the analysis in relation to all sorts of other transference aspects, but the central transactions which I have outlined that are referable to the geographical confusions, have little depressive anxiety attending them.

The splitting, rather, of the object in a severe way takes place and may persevere for a long time, so that the analyst is in effect *only* a toilet and all good things for introjection come from mother, teacher, siblings, friends. This does not mean that an introjective process does not in fact take place, but that it is not acknowledged in the analysis: it is rather, attributed, and indeed experienced, elsewhere. Thus a child may for a long time bring toys, sweets, food or books from home, do homework or knit. The reason for the rigidity of this splitting is clearly to be seen when the split begins to break down and the severe anxieties of soiling, polluting and poisoning the feeding breast become so clear. This is rather beautifully illustrated in *The Narrative* in later sessions when the threat of termination brings it forth with desperate urgency.

This split in the transference amounts to a type of denial of psychic reality and much acting out at home in relation to food may accompany it. Thus it becomes clear that the geographical confusion at this time involves not only a confusion between the inside and outside of the object but also a confusion between external reality and psychic reality. Only with the establishment of the toilet-breast as an object in psychic reality through the repeated experience of it externally in the transference, is the relinquishment of massive projective identification possible, since this mechanism aims at escaping from an unbearable infantile identity. Once this separate identity has thus been made bearable through the modulation of pain, the way is opened for other developmental steps, as I shall discuss in the chapters on subsequent phases in the analytic process.

It is in this phase that we can most graphically see the truth of the great discovery by Melanie Klein, amplified in recent writings by W. R. Bion, that the most primitive form of relief of psychic pain is accomplished by the evacuation into the external object of parts of the self in distress and the persecutory debris of attacked internal objects, receiving back through the introjective aspect the restored objects and relieved parts of the self. In its most concrete form with children actual urination and defecation, using the toilet or, unfortunately on occasions, the consulting room takes place. Most striking is the change in the demeanour of the child at start and finish of such sessions, the relief mixed with contempt with which, without a goodbye, he cheerfully leaves, in contrast with the frantic and disorganised bursting-in type of entry.

I have called this object in the transference the "toilet-breast" because this is its most primitive representation prior to the defence, by horizontal splitting of the mother, which locates the toilet functions below, in connection with her buttocks, while reserving the feeding function for the upper part of the mother's body, breasts, nipples, eyes and mouth — and therefore her mind.

In adult patients the phenomena are more subtle, some of which I have described as the phenomenology of the "pseudo-mature" aspects of the personality, seen in so many cases of borderline or more severe psycho-pathology, in my paper on "Anal Masturbation and Its relation to Projective Identification".

I stress the relation of this phase of geographical confusion of the analytic process particularly to adult cases of borderline or more severe psychopathology since the resolution of this configuration of object relation stands as the border between mental illness (psychosis) and mental health, just as the resolution of the obstacles to the dependent introjective relation to the breast traverses the border between mental instability and mental stability, and as the passing of the oedipus complex leads from immaturity to maturity. It is a phase of analysis which can last for years with very disturbed patients and, in my experience, may not be very satisfactorily resolved at all and prove an intractable resistance where inadequate environmental support renders the analytic breaks intolerable, in children as well as adults. However, while almost endless patience may be required of the analyst in this phase — and tolerance — progress is almost always steadily achieved. The patient who cannot manage it will either break down at a holiday or leave before or after one. This situation, therefore, is one to which the analytic method seems basically adequate and should be distinguished from those we will meet later which more correctly deserve the name of intractable resistances. In other words, if an analyst can bear to persevere when geographical confusions are in the forefront of the transference he will certainly be rewarded with progress, no matter how slow, for this progress is in almost no way dependent on the cooperation of the adult part of the personality. A striking example of this is seen with disturbed adolescents whose primary mode of effecting projective identification may be to miss sessions for prolonged periods or to miss a percentage of each week's sessions. The analyst who can hold on, while managing the technical problems so as not to seem to compound the delinquency toward the parents, will succeed.

As the dominance of geographical confusion recedes from the transference, the mid-week begins to clear and to be dominated in turn by the configuration to which we must now turn attention. But for a very long time in the analysis this pattern of massive projective identification must be expected in the region of every break, especially those outside the analytic routine.

The twenty-odd years of clinical work and teaching since writing the "process" book has seen much to confirm this general formulation, but also many changes in emphasis which might well be mentioned here, although they will emerge more fully later. First, I would no longer like to speak of "massive" projective identification, partly because it is too quantitive a term where quantity of phenomenology may be confused with quantity of underlying personality structures. Experience has shown, particularly in the "Sorting of Zonal Confusions" phase of analysis, that the return to states of mind dominated by projective identification does not by any means represent a return of a part to its sequestered position within an object. On the contrary it often merely signifies a shift in the centre of gravity, at the moment, of the sense of identity without reflecting a structural shift. In a well-established disturbance, as seen in adult character disorders and in psychotic children, the ensconced part of the self does not easily emerge from projective identification until a very substantial healthy structure has been established that can support the strain of its reintegration. This finding is in keeping with Mrs. Klein's description of the difficulties of reintegrating a split-off envious part of the personality described in *Envy and Gratitude*.

41

In restrospect I think the reason for accepting the idea of "massive" and therefore the optimism expressed about the emergence from projective identification was due to neglecting to follow closely the claustrophobic anxieties, while being impressed by the manic and omnipotent identificatory aspects. It was the work of Doreen Weddell with "Barry" which called greater attention to the space itself inside the object and its characteristics, and therefore its emotional impact on the sequestrated part. The slow and painful way in which this autistic boy, no longer very young by any means, gradually discovered the three-dimensional space within himself and his object, and then gradually allowed the inside of his object to become structured and differentiated, opened our eyes to the complicated nature of the projective experience in projective identification, claustrophobia in particular, but claustrophilia in addition. As will be seen later, my remark (p.33) about the "return-to-sleep-inside-mother" as an aspect of projective identification would now be considered doubtful, owing to our recently acquired experiences of echographic study of foetal life.

Finally I would mention a shift in emphasis. The general optimism of the description of analytic progress I would certainly agree with, but not its emphasis on "correct" interpretation. I now consider that interpretation content has very little impact in this phase of analysis and for a very evident reason. Because the behaviour of the patient, adult or child, is so largely in the nature of acting-in-the-transference at this time, the analyst's behaviour, verbal and otherwise, has the impact of actions rather than communications. Therefore factors which generate the atmosphere of the consulting room, what I have pointed out as the management of the temperature and distance of the relationship, would seem to supplement what is here described as the "toilet-breast" functions of the analyst's interest, patience, tolerance and attempts to understand — in a word, containment.

The writing of *Sexual States of Mind* did not come as a rush of intuition as had the *Process*, nor did I have the support of colleagues in working out the ideas as in the case of *Autism*. As the book reflects, it was a slow and piecemeal effort which largely grew out of a careful and systematic study of Freud while on the committee working out a new curriculum at the British Institute of Psycho-analysis. I was greatly impressed by the gap between the commonly held conception of Freud's views on sexuality, as stated in the "Three Essays on Sexuality" (1905) and the many, largely unsystematized statements in later works, particularly those which dissected the polymorphous from the perverse in the sexual disposition and behaviour. All of this seemed to grow in him from reverberations set going by the experience of the "Wolf Man". I described Freud's addenda in the following way in *Sexual States*:

> From what he calls "The Primal Period" Freud traces the following events: the primal scene (during which the baby interrupted the parental coitus by passing a stool); the early eating difficulties brought to an end by the implied danger of death; the early scene with "Grusha" (meaning "pear" in Russian) and its link with enuresis, fire dreams, the butterfly phobia and the later falling in love with servant girls. These form the background of the "Wolf-man's" active and later masculine strivings as well as his tendencies to regression to oral sadism (cannibalism). On the other hand Freud traces the theme of the "Wolf-man's" passivity and its ramifications into his femininity, on the one hand, and his masochism on the other, to the baby's passage of the stool at the primal scene and his later bowel difficulties which were related to his mother's gynaecological troubles. Thus the complaint of impaired sense of reality, relieved only by enemata, is traced to the theme of having been "born with a caul", the narcissistic expectation of eternal good fortune (shattered by gonorrhoea) and his little boy cruelty to small animals representing the mother's internal babies.
>
> The latter passive current of potential anal (vaginal) femininity was altered to passive masculinity (phallic) by his sister's seduction and her tales about Nanya.
>
> From the tracing and reconstruction of this primal scene and its two dominant currents of excitement Freud draws two astonishing conclusions:
>
> (p. 101) "... he wishes he could be back in the womb, not simply in order that he might be reborn, but in order that he might be copulated with there by his father ";

(p. 102) "There is a wish to be back in a situation in which one was in the mother's genitals; and in this connection the man is identifying himself with his own penis ...".

One need only combine these two statements to gain a third implication, namely that in coitus a man may be identified with his own penis as if it were a child inside the mother's genital being there copulated with by the father. Unfortunately the "in the womb" aspect of the masculine and feminine phantasy seems to have got lost between 1914 and 1919, but when Freud returns to the theme again in 1924 in "The Economic Problem of Masochism" he is attempting to relate the problem to the duality of instinct proposed in "Beyond the Pleasure Principle". Accordingly that portion of the Death Instinct which is not directed outward as sadism is seen to be retained as a primary (1°) erotogenic masochism from which two developmental forms, feminine and moral masochism develop, while the "reintrojection" of projected destructiveness can produce a secondary (2°) masochism. This latter can effect a masochistic solution to any "developmental coating" and its associated anxiety, whether it be the fear of being eaten, beaten, castrated or copulated. These conclusions can be recognised to link with an earlier paper on character ("Some Character Types met with in Psycho-analytic Treatment" — S. E., 14, 1916) where Freud had described "those wrecked by success", "criminals from a sense of guilt" and "The exceptions", all three aspects being recognisable in the character of the "wolf-man".

But of even more importance for our consideration here is the category of "feminine masochism", by which Freud meant the "normal" feminine attitude to sexuality in women, or, strangely, the perversion of masochism in men who phantasy or arrange in fact to be tied up, beaten, defiled, abused, etc. (p. 162) "The obvious interpretation, and one easily arrived at, is that the masochist wants to be treated like a small and helpless child, but particularly like a naughty child." But psycho-analytic study reveals the underlying feminine wish "of being castrated, or copulated with, or giving birth to a baby".

Thus the new "notation" of life and death instincts had offered Freud a way of dissecting the phenomenology of masochism into "feminine" and "moral", thus separating those factors related to guilt (moral) from those related to bisexuality (feminine erotogenic masochism in men and women) and also from those developmental forms of masochism (2°) resulting from defensive processes.

Again what I wish to stress is the interplay between deductive and inductive method in the progress of Freud's thinking. What had been an incidental aspect of the "Wolf-man's" reconstructed childhood could now be re-evaluated in the light of a new notation for instinct and psychic structure and used to explore similar aspects of other cases, giving promise of a new theory of the perversions. The projecting and reintrojecting of sadism, the kaleidoscopic shifting of identifications, the flux of bisexuality and the confusion of active-passive aims with masculine-feminine ones of a later developmental level could all begin to be correlated with each other. And the key was clearly the situation of the small child in relation to the primal scene or the primal phantasy.

It was only a short step now to solve the riddle of the fetish (On Fetishism - *S.E.*, 21, 1927) as combining the denial of castration anxiety (the phantasy that the woman does have a penis) and denial of the wish for castration. For again the new structural notation enabled Freud to state that contrary situations could exist side by side in the unconscious by the agency of a "split". This idea had been touched on at various points from the time of the "Project" but had only begun to be given real meaning earlier in the 1924 paper on "Neurosis and Psychosis", and would be amplified later in "Splitting of the Ego in the Process of Defence" (1937) and the "Outline" (1938). The way in which Freud states it in the 1924 paper is particularly germane to the struggles of the "Wolf-man." He says (pp. 152 – 53), "The thesis that neuroses and psychoses originate in the ego's conflicts with its various ruling agencies — that is, therefore, that they reflect a failure in the functioning of the ego, which is at pains to reconcile all the various demands made on it — this thesis needs to be supplemented in one further point. One would like to know in what circumstances and by what means the ego can succeed in emerging from such conflicts, which are certainly always present, without falling ill. This is a new field of research, in which no doubt the most varied factors will come up for examination. Two of them, however, can be stressed at once. In the first place, the outcome of all such situations will undoubtedly depend on economic considerations — on the relative magnitudes of the trends which are struggling with one another; in the second place, it will be possible for the ego to avoid a rupture in any direction by deforming itself, by submitting to encroachments on its own unity and even perhaps effecting a cleavage or division of itself. In this way the inconsistencies, eccentricities and follies of men would appear in a similar light to their sexual perversions, through the acceptance of which they spare themselves repression." '

Thus Freud had come some considerable distance from the facile formula that neuroses were the negative of perversions. The complexity of the perversion and its relation to character had been opened up.

REFERENCES

"A Child is Being Beaten", *S.E.*, 17, 1919.
"Economic Problem of Masochism", *S.E.*, 19, 1924.
"On Fetishism", *S.E.*. 21, 1927.
"From the History of an Infantile Neurosis", *S.E.*, 18,, 1918; Brunswick, R. M., I. J. Psa., 9;439, 1928. Gardiner, M. Publ. Phila. Psa., 2:32, 1952.

(*Sexual States*, Ch. VI)

The support given by these intuitions of Freud to the later findings of Melanie Klein regarding both splitting processes and projective identification strengthened my conviction first of the importance of masturbatory processes and of the phantasies, claustrophobic and claustrophilic, of the space inside the internal maternal object as a life space, a world with its own qualities and values. The paper on "Identification and Socialization in Adolescence" (Chapter VII) made the important link between masturbatory bed-play in latency and gang-formation, giving a firmer form to the concept of "narcissistic organization". At that time I did not clearly see how different this was from Bion's formulation of the Basic Assumption Group.

In rereading *Sexual States*, which was written piecemeal (Elizabeth Spillius rightly said it suffered from "two-hour-itis") between 1965 and 1973, I am surprised how little occupied I was with this spatial aspect, nor had I clearly drawn the phenomenological distinction between the projective and the identificatory consequences of projective identification phantasies. In retrospect, in the consulting room, supervisions and teaching, I seem to have been working out the details of narcissistic organization and its conseqences for development and psychopathology. The differentiations adult/infantile, polymorphous/perverse, good/naughty/bad in sexual behaviour, habitual/addictive/criminal in the perversions, and a broadening of the role of fetishism must have quite preoccupied me, but on the other hand the working out of these structural factors, along with the role of zonal confusions, in the impedence of the entry into a depressive orientation was probably a precondition for a full exploration of the spatial, geographical aspects. Bion's theory of thinking and its connection with his ideas on groups was bit by bit making its impact. At many places it can be seen that I am searching for a way of including concepts of truth and beauty as aspects of psychic reality and of the impact of external objects so that the concept of a bad part of the personality could take on some functional substance. Melanie Klein's description of the phantasied attacks on objects did not in itself embrace the meaning of the attacks, although she carefully explored the motivation behind these onslaughts. Bion's theory of thinking directed attention to this meaning, particularly the idea of attacks-on-linking, the fluidity of Ps↔D. Both Mrs. Klein's adherence to Life and Death Instincts and Bion's evocation of the "foul fiend" aspect of the personality supported the view of absolute evil, for I had not yet taken in the implications of Bion's revision of affect theory, positive and negative Love, Hate and Knowing.

Having undertaken, in 1972 and 1973, to deliver the lectures on Freud and Klein to the pre-clinical students of the Child Psychotherapy Course at the Tavistock Clinic, I found myself confronted with the request to do the same for Bion's work with the advanced students, staff and guests in 1976 and 1977. It was a stroke of fortune to be forced to a systematic review of his life's work, for virtually everything but the *Memoir of the Future* was by then available. The *Kleinian Development* that resulted from these various lecture series need not detain us here, but whatever its virtues and defects, the effort of unwilling scholarship so ordered my own thinking that it certainly marked a watershed in my work between what I could reasonably view as faithful filling in the clinical implications of the work of Melanie Klein and excursions beyond, following, no, utilizing — for there is no possibility of following — Bion's thought. It has been dubbed "Post-Kleinian" and I accept that appelation, for good or ill. I cannot say with any conviction that Mrs. Klein would have been pleased with these ideas, but I know she would have encouraged me — and us, in a certain sense — to go our independent way. For although she could defend her ideas from attack, and vigorously, she was ever alert to lip-service and orthodoxy!

In a certain sense Bion's investigations turned research interest back to the elucidation of ego functions, where Mrs. Klein's preoccupations had been with relationships and personality structuring. Where the play of children had presented itself as the most convincing evidence of the concreteness of psychic reality and the structure of self and objects, the area for the study of mental functions was clearly to be found in the dream-life of adult patients. The Bionic background to *Dream Life*, published in 1983, five years after the *Kleinian Development*, is described there in this way:

Conditions in which particular functions are disordered attracted Wilfred Bion, beginning with his investigation of schizophrenic patients and their difficulties in thinking. By tracing Melanie Klein's concepts of splitting processes and projective identification not only to personality structures, but to separate Ego functions such as thinking, memory, attention, verbalization, action, judgment, he explored the possibility that the mind could attack itself in very minute ways. He adduced evidence of the splitting off of particular mental functions, as well as the projection of bits of the personality containing these isolated functions into other objects. Such objects of projective identification could then be experienced as able to perform these split-off functions, while what was left of the self could no longer perform them. And then, utilizing this concept of minute splitting and projective attacks on the self's capacities, he began to investigate and elaborate a concept of thinking. What he did first was to separate *thoughts*, and the elaboration of thoughts, from *thinking* as the transformation of these thoughts. He then introduced a modification to Melanie Klein's emphasis on the baby's relationship to the breast and the mother as the great modulator of mental pain which enables the baby to proceed with its development.

Under Melanie Klein's model, the development of the mind resembles the unfolding of a flower when it is adequately nourished and free from parasites or predators. Bion took quite a different view; namely that the development of the mind is a complicated process which has to be structured every step of the way and cannot therefore be compared with the biological forms of growth that are determined by genetic history and implemented by hormonal systems. He thought that mental development was in a sense autonomous; that the mind builds itself, bit by bit, by "digesting" experiences.

Bion took the view that the mother has to perform functions for the baby — mental functions — which the baby can then learn to perform for itself by internalizing her. He formulated it in terms of the baby's relationship to the breast: essentially the baby, being in a state of confusion and having emotional experiences about which it cannot think, projects distressed parts of itself into the breast. The mother and her mind (experienced by the baby as her breast), has to perform the function of thinking for the baby. She returns to the baby those disturbed parts of itself in a state that enables thinking, and particularly dreaming, to come into existence. This he called alpha-function. He left it as an "empty" concept because he did not know how to fill it and he was not at all certain that it could be filled in by any substantial description.

This conception of the development of the baby's capacity to think implied that it is not only dependent on the mother's reverie to put order into chaotic experience, but also on her availability as an object for internalization. This has given new significance to the human infant's protracted period of helplessness, so non-adaptive on superficial consideration. By linking dependence with the experience of the absent object as the "first thought", Bion suggested a new, highly adaptive meaning for the long period of infantile helplessness, implying it is necessary for the internalization of the mother as a *thinking* object, not merely as a *serving* one. This gave new meaning to Freud's speculation about Primary Narcissism and new importance to Melanie Klein's dating of the onset of the depressive position.

It must be said that much remained to be digested of Bion's ideas in the following years. Somehow the rich opportunity of seeing cross-cultural material from analyses conducted in various countries of Europe, the U.S., South America and India, which had become open to Martha Harris and myself during the seventies, furthered this evolution in a surprising way. Perhaps it was the requirement of simplicity in exposition in translation to audiences who had read Klein and Bion only partially, and in translation usually, that contributed to a process of condensation and clarification. But also it was the splendid material, so carefully prepared, which constantly added new weight to the fact that an Extended Metapsychology was being fashioned. This, in my view, is the heart of the matter of Post-Kleinian psychology: that to Freud's four categories of exposition — dynamic, genetic, structural and economic — there has been added in increasing detail the investigation of the geographic and epistemological aspects of mental functioning. Whether the Aesthetic aspect will eventually take on sufficient distinctness to add a seventh category remains to be seen.

These experiences involving a wide range of different languages, of which I had, being a poor linguist, either little or no knowledge, had directed my interest in language as early as the research group on autism. In the chapter on "Mutism in Infantile Autism, Schizophrenia and Manic-depressive states", I had defined five distinct factors necessary for the use of words, in combination with the musical-gramatical aspects of language, for communication:

These five factors, which can be seen to operate only singly, in tandem or consortium in mental illness where a tendency to mutism is present, are as follows:
(a) It is necessary for mental functioning to be sufficiently ordered for the formation of dream thoughts suitable for communication by some means, and not merely requiring evacuation (Bion).

(b) There must be an apparatus for transforming dream thought into language; this apparatus consists of internalized speaking objects from whom and in identification with whom (whether by a process of narcissistic or introjective identification) the musical deep grammar for representing states of mind can be learned.

(c) In the early years, when the lalling impulse is still strong, the child must build up a vocabulary for describing the outside world, so that he may develop a virtuosity in super-imposing this surface, lexical, language upon the deeper, musical, language; and so be able to communicate about the outside world.

(d) These internal transformations, inner speech, must find an object in the outside world which has sufficient psychic reality and adequate differentiation from the self, to require the vocalization of this inner process in order for communication to take place.

(e) The desire for communication with other human beings must be sufficient to sustain the continuing process of dream-thought formation.

(Autism, Ch. VII)

This distinction between the communication of information by verbal means and the more unconscious communication of states of mind by projective identification through the music and grammar of speech were thus both seen in the light of transformations of dream-thoughts, equivalent to Melanie Klein's Unconscious Phantasies. Thus "state of mind" was coming to be seen as a momentary manifestation of the functions described by Extended Metapsychology and the dream-thought as its purest, most authentic expression in mental life.

Much of what has been worked out in the recent years regarding the clinical manifestations of Bion's ideas and some of the theoretical implications also has found its way into print in *Studies in Extended Metapsychology* and *The Apprehension of Beauty* (with Meg Harris Williams). But I am abashed to find that very little concerning the projective (or, as I would prefer to call it, the "intrusive") aspects of projective identification has seen the light of publication in English. Since it took the form mainly of lectures that grew out of the various conferences held abroad, it appears only in the publications of those meetings, in French, Italian, Spanish and Norwegian. Hence the necessity, resist it as I have, of publishing this additional burden to our groaning libraries.

Two clinical cases, one heard in Perugia in the late seventies, and one of my own in the early eighties, along with the material of Doreen Weddell's "Barry", awakened my imagination to the qualities and meaning of the world inside an internal maternal object. The case heard in Perugia was of a young man who had stripped himself naked in the middle of his village square and disappeared down the sewer, in order, as he later described, to escape the Gestapo who were seeking to enlist him in their ranks. In the subsequent two years he was in three different mental hospitals, having escaped from the first and second because of intense feelings of persecution. In the first he felt everything was filthy and foul smelling, that tortures were going on whose screams and moans he constantly heard. In the second he complained endlessly of the atmosphere of sexual wantonness among patients and staff which drove him to constant masturbatory excitement. Finally in the third he complained that everything was so beautiful, the air was so sweet-smelling and invigorating, that he could not stop taking deep breaths. In consequence he feared that he was using up too much of the oxygen and might be harming the babies whom he heard crying in the nursery below.

My own patient was a young man who, while working abroad in the industry of some friends of his family, with whom he was also boarding, was overcome with an anxiety state, so delusional that it almost caused his death. He became convinced that, if he greedily ate more food, beyond the monetary value of the work he performed, he would be "slung out". What this expulsion meant he could not say, but it filled him with terror. Consequently he ate less and less, withdrawing from communal meals, and disguised his weight loss by padding his clothes. Finally he became so weak that his deception was discovered and he was sent home by ambulance plane. The fundamentally claustrophobic nature of this delusional state became apparent quickly in the analysis, which was instituted once he recovered his physical health. It became clear that his world was composed of three separate areas or spaces: the consulting room, which was a space of safety and pleasure; his digs, overlooking the deer park of Magdalen College, which was a masturbation-voyeurism chamber; and his place of work as equipment clerk in the basement of a large institution, a place of mild persecution and slavery, where he felt compelled to steal cold food from the kitchen. In his traversing the city en route to and from these spaces, he rushed head down, unseeing to a degree that was perilous in the city traffic.

I will not labour this material but rather bring this review to a close and proceed to the substance of this little book. Just one word about what the following may owe to the careful study of Bion's *Memoir of the Future*. Its illustration of the processes of catastrophic change, and recovery therefrom, has certainly found its way into the fabric of my own imaginative conjectures, and thus my way of experiencing clinical material. But I would draw this distinction. I think Bion has been concerned with catastrophic change as crises in development. With this I agree wholeheartedly. I have probably been more interested in catastrophic change from the point of view of what he has called the moments which hold in suspense the possibilities of both "break-down and break-through". While we probably see many patients in consultation in whom the acute anxieties of this moment are made evident, it is in those who come to us having succumbed to "break-down" that our clearest evidence of the world of the interior of an internal object is derived.

Part 2

3 The Geographic Dimension of the Mental Apparatus

In the model of the mind that I am using the geographical dimension can be subdivided, for phenomenological purposes, into six distinct areas: the external world, the womb, the interior of external objects, the interior of internal objects, the internal world, and the delusional system (geographically speaking "nowhere"). The first five subdivisions comprise areas that have psychic reality. The external world also has a concrete reality which calls forth adaptational processes, fundamentally meaningless. The delusional system is also meaningless in a different way, being delusional in its significances and bizarre in its objects.

To the outside world, beyond our adaptational moves, which are learned largely by infra-mental processes of mimicry (one dimensional) and trial-and-error, we may deploy meaning when the impact of events and objects impinges on us emotionally and are subjected to processes of imagination, that is, to symbol formation (alpha function) and thinking. But we are not limited in this matter to the impact of events and objects; we also have the capacity to deploy emotion and thus infuse with meaning, potentially, events and objects whose impact is not in themselves substantial. In *The Apprehension of Beauty* I proposed a terminology which grows out of Bion's affect theory, plus and minus L (love), H (hate) and K (interest, knowing). I suggested that our innate response to the beauty-of-the-world, that is aesthetic responsiveness, contains an integration of all three of these positive links, L, H and K, but that the pain of the ambivalence combined with the necessity of tolerating uncertainty, makes it very difficult to hold these links together. The splitting processes bring relief by deploying the links to separate objects, thus also splitting the self in its emotional capabilities and experiences. These splitting processes do not necessarily reduce the experiences to an adaptational level — in which thinking about meaning, which necessarily includes value, would be replaced by scheming, logic derived from basic assumptions, and actions aimed at success (triumph).

Where meaningfulness can be preserved despite the splitting of the passionate links, we are in the realm of Melanie Klein's paranoid-schizoid position in terms of values, but the processes of projection and introjection remain active. Modification becomes possible, because action can be restrained in favour of thought. But this commerce between external world experience and internal world processes is dependent on observation and the restraint of premature intellection and story making. Unconscious dream thoughts must be given time to form so that thinking and transformations can occur. The contained must be allowed to enter the container, in Bion's model.

Certain types of clinical experience, when combined with what can be learned from baby observation and echography, suggest that emotional experiences and rudimentary symbol formation and thought commence in the latter months of gestation and form the background upon which the experience with the world outside, and in particular the first encounters with the mother's body and mind, make their crucial impact. Bion's suggestion that infantile parts may be left behind at birth, remain enwombed, is strongly suggested in patients in whom a traumatic factor complicates their gestation: maternal illness, infarction of the placenta, prematurity, foetal distress, to name a few. This is an area still to be worked out: its impact on character, its appearance as states of withdrawal, its part in sleep patterns. I mention it here to distinguish it from those aspects of projective (intrusive) identification with which this book is so particularly concerned.

These states of mind, whether central to the character or only contributory, require division into two categories: those contingent upon intrusion or those resulting from passive induction into external objects. These latter seem to result in various pathological states such as folie à deux, multiple personality, demoniacal possession. Where an external object carries infantile transference, introjection easily ensues on separation. None of these states seem to concern us here for they all present primarily identificatory manifestations of a narcissistic type, without the claustrophobic phenomena.

But the intrusive indentification with internal objects seems always to show both aspects, the identificatory and the pro-jective (claustrophobic). The internal object of these processes is par excellence the internal maternal object and its special compartmentalization. Where projection into the internal paternal object is obtrusive, it seems to be as a means of entry to the mother's body. It has important identificatory consequences but little of the claustrophobic in its own right. These identificatory aspects, of projective identification with internal and external objects, have been extensively studied. It is almost exclusively the intrusive, projective ones that concern us here, from the theoretical viewpoint, while their intermingling in the clinical situation will concern us with regard to the technical problems.

All of these considerations require differentiation from the relationships of the self to its internal objects insofar as their boundaries of inviolable individuality and privacy are respected at all levels. I think it fair to say that internal objects impinge on the self, at various levels, because of both their qualities and their functions. Unlike external objects, emotions are not deployed to these objects, they are evoked by them. It is at this level of psychic reality that form and function are experienced as wedded so that beauty is truth, truth beauty.

As the various children of a single family discover eventually that, experientially, they have "different" parents, so it is that the different parts of the self have different internal objects. For some parts of the self objects are at a partial object level, for others they are invaded and altered by projections; for some the paternal and maternal are far apart while for others they are combined; for some they are held under omnipotent control, while other parts of the self can give their internal objects their freedom. From this point of view reintegration of the self is contingent upon the reintegration, in a sense the rehabilitation, of the internal objects. And upon this integration the further development of the internal objects becomes a possibility, going beyond what Freud envisioned as their accruing qualities from outside the family, from heroes and heroines of the present and past. The integrated internal combined object learns from experience in advance of the self and is almost certainly the fountainhead of creative thought and imagination.

In pitiful contrast to the glorious possibilities of growth for self and objects which the links of positive LH and K embrace, the anti-life and anti-emotion forces which dedicate themselves to minus LH and K, to puritanism, hypocrisy and Philistinism, construct a Pandemonium of the delusional system. Their tools are stupid, essentially. Negative mimicry builds a world of delusional ideas and bizarre objects from the debris of alpha-function-in-reverse, aided by transformations in hallucinosis and the format of the negative grid. This would seem to be the Bionic formulation whose evocation clinically we cannot pause to consider here. It will have some mention in Chapter 8 on the Role of the Claustrum in the Onset of Schizophrenia.

4   The Compartments of the Internal
         Mother

Although the clinical realizations which gave rise to the
conception of the compartmentalization of the internal
mother's body go back to the early 1960's, the autism research
group that finally produced *Explorations in Autism*, and
particularly to the late Doreen Weddell's work with "Barry", it
was not until twenty years later that the full significance came
through to me. Out of clinical work and teaching and the
literary companionship of Martha Harris and her daughters the
conception of aesthetic conflict arose to alter considerably my
view of personality development and the human condition. In
between came the various essays collected and organized in
Sexual States of Mind where the internal compartmentalization of
the internal mother's body, its reference to orifices and the
polymorphous nature of adult sexuality, added substance to the
formal description.

It is clear that two new ideas which, by gaining clarity, made
the descriptions in this present book possible, are Bion's affect
theory, plus and minus L, H and K, and the central part in the
oscillations Ps↔D, played by the aesthetic conflict. In seeing this
as a tormenting uncertainty about the interior qualities of the
aesthetic object, it becomes possible to express the idea of ego
strength as negative capability. When the dimension strength/
weakness becomes thus observable in its operation and not
merely construed from its consequences, we seem to move to a
new level of precision in clinical observation (and self-scrutiny).

What emerges in the consulting room and in supervisions is
a greatly clarified distinction between immaturity and psychopathology. On the one hand one can range the manifestations of
infantile confusions of both a geographic and zonal nature along
with Money-Kyrle's thesis of developmental misconceptions.
In contrast to this are the pathological constructions which arise ·
from what Bion calls "lies" or column 2 of the grid, failure of
alpha-function perhaps induced by what I have called "story-
telling" reversal of alpha-function with a debris (beta-elements-
with-traces-of-ego-and-superego) from which bizarre objects

and the delusional system are shaped by the forces of minus LHK, and finally the operation of omnipotent mechanisms (splitting processes, omnipotent control of objects and intrusive identification).

From the point of view of model-of-the-mind, it is necessary to trace development both in terms of self and of objects. My own emphasis previously, along with the general trend in Kleinian descriptions, has been on the evolution of the self, particularly from the structural aspect. Here, where we are attempting an exploration of the consequences of the intrusive side of the dual phenomena of projective identification, we need to attempt ¡a description primarily of the geography and qualities of the internal objects and secondarily to trace the metapsychological implications for the self. This latter consideration will include the consequences for structure of the self and also for its view-of-the-world. As a basis for our central investigation into the implications for the internal objects and for the self of the operation of the intrusive side of projective identification as an aspect of psycho-pathology, we need first to clarify the direction and extrapolation of the evolution of the internal objects during the maturational process in order to understand the distortions in objects and self consequent to the intrusion.

The first thing that must be clarified is the difference between a conception of the inside of the internal mother derived from imagination and one that is the product of the omnipotent intrusion, and thereby of omniscience. Clinical material is able to be quite explicit and precise in regard to the latter, but the former, the interior of the mother as construed from the outside, respecting the privacy of her interior, must be a product of the patient's and the analyst's imagination. But we have another source as well, that given to us by artists and poets. From clinical material one can see that the functions of the different parts of the mother carry an assumption of interior structure, but here of course the forms are borrowed by imagination from those of the outside world. This borrowing of forms has a reflexive consequence for our construing the meaning of the outside world from which the forms have been borrowed. By contrasting the two views — that constructed by imagination and that "discovered" by intrusion — we can also gain a meaningful differential of views-of-the-world as they are determined by psychic reality, in health and in disturbance. The pathological consequences will be discussed in Chapter 5 on Life in the Claustrum.

Here it would be most useful to outline the direction of development of the internal objects insofar as it is reflected in the imaginative conception of the inside of the internal mother. The general movement is clearly from a vast space, undifferentiated and simply containing all forms of life — the Earth Mother — to a compartmentalized but largely partial object mother whose functions for the child (augmented by desires aroused in the child) determine its imaginative constructions. This unintegrated interior is formed in clusters around the assumption of analogy between the infant's experiences of his own orifices vis à vis the mother's services. Thus are eyes drawn to eyes, ears to the mother's mouth, baby mouth to the nipples, nose to the mother's aroma; and thus is the baby's integration gradually brought together into consensuality by the mother's integrated behaviour: baby head to maternal head/breast. But a correspondingly integrated conception of her interior must be a far more difficult task, hampered by both ambivalence aroused by failures in her functions and the aesthetic conflict about the uncertainty of her interior. Particularly is this true of the more problematic areas of excretory processes and erotic genital trends. Probably the desires to penetrate and be penetrated inherent in all orifices greatly complicate the baby's acceptance of dependence for services to these highly erogenous zones. The anxieties about emptying the mother or poisoning her with excrements form a contrapuntal arrangement to the possessiveness and tyrannical trends. It is this mother-in-danger which presses the child away from viewing the father as a rival towards enlisting him for the preservation of this indispensable and treasured object. Of the three orifices assumed open to the father, his functions in feeding and cleaning the mother are more easily accepted than his genital baby-nurturing one. And thus the genital oedipal conflict can hardly be joined until the pregenital ones have been largely resolved.

The consequence of this difficulty in integrating the functions of the mother, insofar as they influence the baby's imaginative conception of her interior, predispose to the image of three compartments in relative or absolute isolation from one another. The inside babies must neither get at the food of the breast nor occupy the mother's thoughts; the rectal rubbish bin must not spill into the breast nor poison the babies in the genital. The forms chosen to represent these compartments and their functions must be borrowed from what is observable of family life, and family life is reflexively imbued with the meaning of these compartments and the anxieties attendant. Thus there ensues a continual commerce between outer world and inner world, a commerce in which the formal qualities are introjected and the meaning externalized. The route of the extrapolation in the maturational process is clearly towards integration and the combined object. But to give substance to these generalizations, we must turn to the artists and poets:

'Beneath him with new wonder now he views
To all delight of human sense expos'd
In narrow room Natures whole wealth, yea more,
A Heav'n on Earth: for blissful Paradise
Of God the Garden was, by him in the East
Of *Eden* planted; *Eden* stretched her Line
From *Auran* Eastward to the Royal Towrs
Of great *Seleucia*, built by *Grecian* Kings,
Or where the Sons of *Eden* long before
Dwelt in *Telassar*: in this pleasant soile
His farr more pleasant Garden God ordained;
Out of the fertil ground he caus'd to grow
All Trees of noblest kind for sight, smell, taste;
And all amid them stood the Tree of Life,
High eminent, blooming Ambrosial Fruit
Of vegetable Gold; and next to Life
Our Death the Tree of Knowledge grew fast by,
Knowledge of Good bought dear by knowing ill.
Southward through *Eden* went a River large,
Nor chang'd his course, but through the shaggie hill
Pass'd underneath ingulft, for God had thrown
That Mountain as his Garden mould high rais'd
Upon the rapid current, which through veins
Of porous Earth with kindly thirst up drawn,

Rose a fresh Fountain, and with many a rill
Waterd the Garden; thence united fell
Down the steep glade, and met the neather Flood,
Which from his darksom passage now appeers,
And now divided into four main Streams,
Runs divers, wandring many a famous Realme
And Country whereof here needs no account.'

(*Paradise Lost, IV.* 205-35)

The geography of the Garden, originally raised by God for his own pleasure and in which he is wont to walk, is of this strange construction, that a hill has been raised above a river, thus making it an underground river which reappears "from his darksom passages" to unite with the rills which had risen from the fountain on top of the mountain, whose waters had been "through veins of porous earth with kindly thirst up drawn". Reunited, the flood is then divided into four main streams which "runs divers, wandering many a famous Realme/And Country whereof here needs no account". This imaginary vascular system clearly is only of interest to Milton insofar as it nourishes the breasts and head, the Tree of Life "High eminent, blooming Ambrosial Fruit/Of vegetable Gold; and next to Life/Our Death the Tree of Knowledge grew fast by".

It is a powerful invocation of the interior of the mother's body and the separate motives which draw the intruding part of the personality inwards, into the sensual delight of the breast or the omniscience of the mother's (library) head. Of the two it is only the Tree of Knowledge that is forbidden and consequently it is to the longing for Godlike knowledge that Satan appeals in his seduction of Eve. Homer's view of sexuality is less guilt-ridden:

'This hand the wonder framed; an olive spread
Full in the court its ever verdant head.
Vast as some mighty column's bulk, on high
The huge trunk rose, and heaved into the sky;
Around the tree I raised a nuptial bower,
And roofed defensive of the storm and shower;
The spacious valve, with art inwrought, conjoins;
And the fair dome with polished marble shines.
I lopp'd the branchy head; aloft in twain
Sever'd the bole, and smooth'd the shining grain;

65

> Then posts, capacious of the frame, I raised,
> And bore it, regular, from space to space:
> Athwart the frame, at equal distance lie
> Thongs of tough hides, that boast a purple dye;
> Then polished the whole, the finished mould
> With silver shone, with elephant and gold."
>
> (*The Odyssey*, Book XXIII
> (Pope's translation)

Here the voice of the poet evokes for us the nuptial chamber. Again we see the tree, this time the olive, around which this indestructible and sequestered haven is constructed.

But the Odyssey is also a compelling image of the function of the internal father on his return, through the act of love, to rid the internal mother of the persecutors and projected rubbish of the bad and naughty children. This debris, collected in the mother's rectum and removed by the internal father as a Herculean task like the Augean Stable, makes another point at which the relationship of the external parents supports or weakens the child's unconscious concept of the relationship between the internal parents at partial and whole object levels.

These descriptions, taken, as it were, from the vertex of the Telemachus part of the infantile personality vis à vis the bad and naughty brothers and sisters, fraught of course with savage infantile competitiveness, represent the consequences of splitting and idealization of the objects. The "bad" parents are represented as well in phantasy, and in the *Odyssey* they can be found in other aspects of both Ulysses and Penelope. He is the adventurer who stays too long away from the home and is soon off again on his travels. Penelope is also the bad mother whose weakness, unsupported, finds recourse to deception and placation in dealing with the bad children (of the narcissistic gang). But even in their "badness" the idealized parents illustrate the goodness to which, unhampered by infantile projective identifications (of adolescent qualities, for instance in Ulysses and Penelope), the internal objects can develop. The firm establishment of the compartmentalization would seem to be the precondition for the evolution of the qualities of mind of these parental figures, extrapolating to the infinity of truthfulness, goodness and wisdom — to godhead.

The following chapters will explore the alterations wrought in these compartments by the intruding parts of the self. But I cannot leave this tribute to the inspiration coming from the poets and artists without mentioning the great display of this compartmentalization seen through the sin-racked and plague-tormented mentality of the end of the fifteenth century. Bosch's triptych, usually called "The Garden of Earthly Delights", displays the indolence, the sensuality and the claustrophobia of the three compartments consequent to the "first disobedience", the intrusion upon the parental prerogatives.

5   Life in the Claustrum

From the vertex of the Klein/Bion (post-Kleinian) model-of-the-mind, psychopathology can be classified in a way that corresponds well to the purely descriptive classifications of psychiatry. Metapsychological, or rather Extended Meta-psychological, classification would divide into neurotic or psychotic disturbances: paranoid-schizoid struggles (Ps↔D), would contrast with structures effected by splitting and projective identification deeply influencing character, sense of identity, capacity for symbol formation, view-of-the-world, concept formation (cognitive development), mood. In this view the schizophrenias must be set aside as life in a world of the delusional system, beyond contact or commerce with psychic reality.

While we catch fleeting glimpses of life in the claustrum from neurotic and normal patients, it is in work with borderline and psychotic states that the interior world is laid out for our inspection at leisure. Without Bion's Theory of Thinking and Theory of Groups, armed only with Freudian mechanics and Kleinian positions, even with the addition of splitting concepts, our description of these mental states lacks power and vividness, and our therapeutic intervention finds little foothold in the massive wall of resistance to change. The technical problems, which led Freud to consider that the Narcissistic Neuroses were beyond the scope of psycho-analysis for want of a capacity to form a transference, will be considered in the next chapter. Melanie Klein's anchoring of the epistemophilic instinct in the baby's interest in the interior of the mother's body, and therefore of her mind, has been extensively explored in *The Apprehension of Beauty*, and some of the qualities of the interior world as an aspect of psychic reality have already been described in Chapters 2 and 3, as derived from psycho-analysis and the insights of artists. These qualities, construed rather than observed, must be differentiated from those directly experienced through projective identification. These latter, with which we are about to deal, are greatly influenced by the fact of the intrusion. Not only do the motives of the incursion alter the judgment, but the damage done by the parasitism alters the state of the object. This is most clearly seen in the manic-depressive states and in hypochondria, and have been vividly described by Abraham and Mrs. Klein.

Bion's differentiation between communicative and intrusive projective identificatory processes, in its application to external objects, may be taken as a reflection of internal processes, while reserving the influence that the external experiences have upon the qualities of internal objects through the mysterious introjective events. Upon this field of operation the value of the psycho-analytical procedure largely depends for its capacity to rehabilitate damaged internal objects, the so-called "corrective emotional experience" aspect of the process. The crucial role of the object of infantile dependence, essentially internal and reflected outwards in the transference, in inviting and containing projective identifications, experienced as the countertransference, forestalls the intrusive intention to some degree in the presence of the object. But it may fail to do so in the internal situation during separations, as documented by dreams and their sequellae (acting-in, acting out, impairment of contact).

This factor of invitation, and consequently of receptivity, is crucial in object relationships. But it has a perverse counterpart, which must be mentioned in passing in order to set aside its phenomena to avoid confusion with the events with which we are dealing. I am referring to the passive experience of projective identification, of being sucked into the claustrum with both its identificatory and claustrophobic consequences. This is a major factor in those entwinements of parent and child known as folies à deux in their extreme form, but also playing a role in situations where a parent's ambitions for a child exceed an ordinary concerned attitude and have taken on the precise form either of demanding mimicry or of fulfilment of the unrealized ambitions of the parent.

Having clarified the field of discussion of life-in-the-claustrum by excluding communicative projective identi-fication and passive projective processes, we can move onto the business of description of the interior world as experienced from the inside, and the qualities of adaptation that this imposes on the intruder. The description that follows is a composite of clinical experiences over the past fifteen years, following the realizations of "The Delusion of Clarity of Insight", some with my own patients but many from supervisions of the work of young analysts and psychotherapists at home and abroad. More detailed clinical material is sprinkled through earlier publications, particularly the *Studies in Extended Metapsychology* and *The Apprehension of Beauty* (with Meg Harris Williams).

The plan is to work our way from top to bottom, leading into the following chapter on the role of projective identification in specific clinical areas including the onset of schizophrenic illness. But a few generalizations can be made initially which cover the phenomena of all three compartments. The first consideration must deal with modes of entry into the portal, which vary from violence to stealth and trickery when enacted with an external object of infantile transference. To "worm one's way" into someone's confidence, to intrude by eavesdropping and spying into another's privacy, to impose oneself on the thought processes of another by lies and threats, to bind a person in submission by pseudo-generosity coupled with threats of foreclosure — the devices are myriad for insinuating into the mind of the other. These processes with external objects draw their omnipotence, however, from internal object relations and the masturbatory mode, for it is the masturbation which not only accompanies the unconscious phantasy but by the orgiastic climax seals its omnipotence. The conscious masturbatory phantasy often has little direct connection and is merely consciously employed to whip up the excitement and to screen the unconscious process. However it must be said that it is the enactment of the masturbation phantasy with another or group in the outside world that creates a daunting depressive problem. This acts as a seal on the claustrum, as we will see when we investigate the events surrounding the emergence from the interior of the object.

The portals of entry for communicative projection are limited, at the infantile level, to the special senses of the object and non-erotic areas of the skin. But every sense and orifice is a potential portal for the intruder. The eyes can be entered by exhibition, the ears by lies, the nose by flatus, the mouth by contraband morsels, the skin by pinching and picking and scratching, anus, urethra and genital by fingers and objects. The degree of criminality seems to vary over a spectrum ranging from violence to trickery, but somehow the worst, the least forgivable, is the seducer who misuses the invitation to communication for intrusive purposes. This form of criminality is found in pure culture in the psychopath who is ever busy projecting his paranoia. These aspects of degree of criminality have an important impact on the reversibility of the intrusion, and are a vital consideration in the therapy of states engendered by projective identification.

One further generalization is in order: a reminder, as it were, that the intruding part of the personality suffers from anxieties that are contingent on the fact of being uninvited. He is a trespasser, an imposter, a poseur, a fraud, potentially a traitor. But he is also an exile from the world of intimacy, from the beauty of the world, which at best he can see, hear, smell, taste only second-hand through the medium of the object.

It will have been noticed that I am paying very little attention to processes of intrusive identification with the father, internal or external. The reason for this is a simple one. Such intrusions seem to be essentially steps on the way to intrusion into the maternal object, whether they involve the paternal genital or mind. In consequence they do not in themselves produce the state of mind that is under examination but merely implement it.

LIFE INSIDE THE MATERNAL HEAD/BREAST

Construed from outside, the mother head/breast is seen as an object, partial or later integrated with other aspects of the whole mother, eventually as a combined object, nipple/eyes and breast/head, whose primary quality is richness. This richness, at first concrete and related to urgent need for nourishment, becomes diversified in its nuances: generosity, receptiveness, aesthetic reciprocity; understanding and all possible knowledge; the locus of symbol formation, and thus of art, poetry, imagination. Seen from the inside, influenced by the motives for the intrusion, the story is a very different one. Generosity becomes quid pro quo, receptiveness becomes inveiglement, reciprocity becomes collusion, understanding becomes penetration of secrets, knowledge becomes information, symbol formation becomes metonymy, art becomes fashion. Seen from outside, the mother's head/breast is industrious, burdened with responsibilities, prudent from foresight. Viewed from inside it is indolent, carefree, living only in the power of its momentary beauty and wealth.

This vulgarization of concepts therefore characterizes the identificatory grandiosity of the intrusive identification. Where the character is strongly influenced by the identification, we recognize easily the self-styled genius, the critic, the connoisseur, the aesthete, the professional beauty, the rich man, the know-it-all, the scramblers after fame and the "bubble reputation". The secret lives of such people reveal the claustrophobic aspect. They are haunted by the sense of fraudulence and yet cannot see in what way they are different from anyone else of similar social status. They are therefore intolerant of criticism and deeply ineducable, in that they cannot bear teachers. Instead they seek to attach themselves as acolytes aspiring to apostolic status, caricaturing Milton's aspiration to "reconcile the ways of God to men". Their essential indolence is belied by the vitality they will expend getting something for nothing, for anything other than manual labour is suspected of fraudulence. Lacking the capacity for thought and judgment, they are slaves to fashion but know of nothing else. Whatever emotional orientation appears as fashionable they strive to participate in, but without conviction, for their emotions lack immediacy as their actions lack resolution. These emotional failures must be covered by cynicism and mockery, for they have no values other than the opinion of others, especially of the mass of strangers, the crowd, of whom they are deeply terrified and from whom they are alienated by elitism. It is the Proustian world.

Because the life-in-the-claustrum of this compartment plays an important role in the early period of psycho-analytic therapy, particularly with the highly educated and with many adolescents, it seems, apposite to include here the paper which represented for me a breakthrough into the inner workings of omniscience. I have called this particular type of omniscience, to separate it from other categories based on delusional objects and hallocinosis, "The Delusion of Clarity of Insight":

To implement his sensory equipment, tool-making man became scientific-man and developed an astonishing range of instruments for evaluating qualities and quantities in the external world. He developed an adequate notational system for assisting his memory and communication about these objects. Emboldened by this signal success, in the last century particularly, he began to try, with understandable optimism, to apply these same techniques to the description and measurement of the things of which his inner world, psychic reality, is composed.

The consequent output of instruments and data has again been impressive, but many 'people feel uneasy about the value and precision of these products, for in some way they seem to fall so short in richness as well as meaningfulness, of the instruments for investigation and communication developed by poets, artists, musicians and theological figures. Some people feel that it is the conceptual background that is to blame and not the instruments. Others feel that we have come up against the limitations of language, trying, as Wittgenstein (1953) claims, to say things that can only be shown. Freud noted (Breuer & Freud, 1893–5) quite early a very striking split in his own use of language, that his theories rang of the laboratory and his data read like short stories. As he went on with his work he also noted over and over that, when faced with conceptual impasse, he found himself returning to the dream as his primary datum (Freud, 1918).

This seems to be a lesson of which it is easy to lose sight. We can forget that our patients, and ourselves, present a unique language in dreams, a language whose substance shapes the content, if not the aesthetic essence, of art. Dreams borrow the forms of the external world and suffuse them with the meaning of the internal world. We do, with practice, learn to read this dream-language in ourselves and our patients with some fluency, even at times with virtuosity. With its help we find a vocabulary and a music for inter- pretation that are at once highly personal and mysteriously universal. Our use of this dream-pallette underlies the claim

Presented at the 29th International Psycho-Analytical Congress, London, July 1975. Published in the *Int. J. Psycho-anal.* (1976) 57,141 that psychoanalysis is truly an art-form, in itself, quite outside the question of whether any of us are good, let alone great, artificers in its employment. In this method we operate with intuitive insights supervised by scientific, conscious modes of observation and thought. It is a method which is rich enough in its potentialities to allow for the possibility of inspiration and great beauty to emerge.

In this artistic activity supervised by scientific functions the latter are deployed in several echelons. First perhaps we try to see that a formulation 'covers' the material at hand. Then, in repose, we may estimate its harmony with previous material and interpretation. Subsequently we estimate its consequences for the emergence of new material and the evolution of a process. But our strength of conviction does not, I suggest, come from this wedding of insight and judgment. It comes rather from the aesthetic component of the experience, the 'beauty' with which the material and the formulation cohabit, blossom, fruit, as a thing apart from ourselves.

In this slow process the richness with which interpretive possibilities arise in an analyst's mind plays a paradoxical role. While this richness lengthens the time span over which conviction must ripen and beauty emerge, the durability of the conviction is proportionately enhanced. But we can notice times at which quite another process takes place in ourselves, one which we may even confuse with inspiration. Naturally it comes more readily to our notice in our patients and I have come to think of it as the 'delusion of clarity of insight'. It, too, bears offspring, but not ones of beauty. Its favourite child is called 'sitting-in-judgment'. Others such as smugness, superciliousness, aloofness and pride follow quickly on.

It is just this juxtaposition and the basis of shifting between these two types of functioning that I wish to explore and exemplify, for I suspect that identification processes and the shift from introjective to narcissistic modes, are at its root. I say 'narcissistic' identifications rather than 'projective' identification (Klein, 1946) because I am not at all sure that the latter is the only means of its, the shift's, achievement. But as you will see, my material points only to a specific aspect of projective identification, one which is bound up

75

closely with the epistemophilic instinct. Where the thirst for knowledge is still strongly dominated by motives related to envy and jealousy, the thirst for knowledge is impatient of learning either from experience, example or demonstration. It seeks rather the immediate emotional satisfaction of omniscience and this it accomplishes by intruding inside the sensory apparatus and mental equipment of its internal object. Here are three clinical vignettes to illustrate this:

Case A.

A medical student had noticed recently a sharp deterioration in his capacity for clinical observation and thought during the course of an analytical break. He brought a dream that *he and his wife were walking along a country road admiring the scenery, and then they were driving in a car along a causeway between two bodies of water. Suddenly the car stopped and he realized that he had gone too far and had broken off the rubber hose which connected his car to the petrol pump.*

The point of the dream seems to be that when he is in projective identification (driving the car) his appreciation of the complexity and beauty of his data (the landscape) is narrowed to one-track-mindedness and simple ideas of causality (the causeway) until he recognizes the need for the analysis (fuel pump) to help him get beyond his present limitations.

Case B.

A young author in the fifth year of his analysis was struggling with his genital Oedipus conflict, his dependence upon the analysis and upon his internal objects for the continuation of his creative powers. The prospect of termination of the analysis had come in sight and tended to throw him into a confusion of identity with his little daughter and the problem of having a second child. He dreamed that *he was with a colleague* (long recognized to be linked to the analyst) *inside a dome-like conservatory* (like the one he had been admiring near the Heath the previous day) *discussing his new book. When the colleague suggested that the two main sections of the book should be more creatively linked together in a geographical way, the patient was suddenly disturbed by a droning sound. When he looked up the sky was crowded with transparent objects, a mixture of Luftwaffe and fireflies. He felt he must rush home to protect his little girl from the bombs.*

It seemed strongly to imply that the moment the analyst suggests that his internal objects might be allowed to come together to create a new baby, the patient's delusion-of-clarity-of-insight (inside the conservatory-breast) recognizes that this would be dangerously destructive to the little girl part of himself and that she must be protected from such an experience at all costs. It would only bombard her with Nazi-envy and preoccupation with daddy's exciting genitals (fireflies).

Case C.

A young woman seemed unable to make any progress in analysis because of shallowness of a latency-period type in which she was waiting-for-daddy-to-come-to-marry-her. This had firmly attached itself to the analyst-daddy in such a way that no interpretation was taken seriously for its content but only as a countertransference activity expressing either loving or sadistic erotism. After visiting her brother's family for the weekend she dreamed that *she was taking a little boy up in a lift and kissing him, but she was somewhat afraid that her breath might smell bad.* This dream was construed to mean that she had got inside the analyst-mummy at the weekend to steal her babies but was worried that her love was contaminated by her anal sadism reflected in her addiction to smoking.

The following night she dreamed that *she was inside a glass conservatory protecting a little boy from Cary Grant, who seemed to be a raving homo-sexual intent on whipping the boy with his extraordinarily long penis.* As I interpreted to her at some length (sic!) that she had shifted from stealing the babies from the mummy to being one of these inside-babies masochistically submitted to the sadistic tongue-penis of the erotic daddy, the patient mainly giggled and smirked and asked why I was so serious, why was I so excited, that my interpretation seemed disappointingly unoriginal, that I was probably hurt by her lack of admiration for my mind, etc.

Clearly I was unable to shift her from her state of projective identification inside the breast (conservatory) from which position the delusion-of-clarity-of-insight into the analyst's state of mind showed her unequivocally that he was hurt, excited, and sadistically whipping her with long interpretation-penises.

Clearly such examples are too anecdotal and unconvincing. They can only exemplify, leaving many doubts and unanswered questions. The broad landscape narrowing to the causeway may suggest an impoverished imagination in Case A. The simplification of modes of thought from complex linking to simple causality may be implied. The dome-shaped conservatory suggests the breast and the transparency of the Luftwaffe-fireflies may indeed imply a high degree of omniscience in Case B. The fact that Case C. is dependent on her spectacles to a degree that far outstrips her refractive error may be linked with going up in the lift, as a means of getting inside the mother's conservatory head-breast to look at the world through her eyes. But it is all only suggestive on its own. To find greater conviction as well as a richer conception of the role of such operations in a person's life-style we must look at a more longitudinal picture of an analysis.

Case D.

This handsome woman in her 40s was well along in her career as a research chemist, successfully combined with marriage and children, when she came to analysis in some despair about her bad temper with the children, picking at her forehead and compulsive eating of chocolate. Her relationship with Mr D. seemed to have progressively deteriorated since they had spent an extraordinarily happy and fruitful year in Canada, each working in their somewhat related fields. From the outset she was extremely sceptical about analysis and felt that, of the many people she knew in London who had been analysed, the only one who showed distinct improvement in Mrs D.'s eyes was paradoxically the least enthusiastic about the method.

From the outset the work was continually confronted by a

minute questioning of the validity of the method by this highly intelligent and observant woman. It was not done in a hostile way but was presented as necessary to her giving a more faultless cooperation. This indeed she did, super-ficially, but her attitudes suggested an underlying negativism and she admitted feeling little hope of benefit. However, she felt she could not resign herself in good conscience to the peculiarities of her character, since they affected the children, not to mention her husband's happiness, until every reason-able effort had been made. In a sense the analyst had to maintain the working-level of hopefulness and bear the full burden of the hopelessness which constantly recurred. He and analysis were put to the test while the patient waited with rather exquisitely balanced wishes for the distant outcome. When it transpired that the presenting complaints were only small fragments of her character and symptom pathology, no improvement in other areas was granted status. Her irrit-ability only grew worse until it finally metamorphosed by the third year into a diffuse indifference and lovelessness towards everyone. In her tally-book the analysis had only made her worse and indeed gave every promise of completely wrecking her life. Yet, paradoxically, she had no desire to leave, but rather showed every sign of settling in for the duration — of her or my life, whichever was the shorter. In the face of this daunting loss of interest — in work, children, sexuality, social life — it was necessary to hold fast to the rigging of the analysis and its internal evolution.

But in fact the development of the analytical material, the evolution of the transference and the patient's growing understanding of mental processes left nothing to be desired, except for pleasure and enthusiasm on her part. An early intense erotic transference had exhibited very clear voyeurist elements. A strong desire to look at the analyst, minute monitoring of his noises, smells and appearance as well as those of the rest of the house, all accompanied by intense oceanic emotionality at times, seemed, as illustrated by her dreams, to point to the impact of early experiences in the parental bedroom. Secretiveness proliferated, along with a rather paranoid attitude about the possibility of being recognized going to or coming from the analyst's rooms. She kept the analysis an absolute secret from her mother, despite the fact that their relations had grown very warm, replacing the custodial posture Mrs D. had adopted since her father's death. When it was suggested that this secretiveness must be part of a diffusely hurtful demeanour to her mother, the patient tried to establish that this was not the case. When her questions to her mother were answered by, 'Well I know you love me', Mrs D. could not see the resignation implied. In fact the evidence all pointed in the direction of her having been a child of some sinew, with whom a technique of compromise had been early adopted. Her obstinacy was immense and could easily have been driven to self-destructive activity if not appeased. In addition she had held her little sister hostage in many ways. In the transference situation it was clear that her need to be 'right' was an overriding passion and could be traced back with some conviction to the conjoint events of her second year: birth of the sister, moving out of the parental bedroom, and move to a new house.

The erotic relation to the analyst as combined parents repeated in great detail the blissful period in the parents' bedroom and its attendant confusion of identity (Meltzer, 1967). It seemed clear from dreams that the year abroad in Canada had been similarly experienced in the depths so that the return to London had stirred recollections of the great expulsion, never forgiven. Her revenge on her parents in childhood had taken the form of arrogating to herself a very sanctimonious secrecy regarding her sexuality, which was meant to parallel the establishment of the privacy of their bedroom. She became a child who confided everything else as a screen for this breach of faith and, for a long time after the erotic transference subsided, this double standard of confidentiality reappeared in the analytic situation. But gradually her dreams gave away its content of a rather diffuse anal perversity. Its enactment in her marriage was revealed and a disengagement from it was slowly effected.

In consequence of this the analytical separations were felt more keenly and this made it possible for a clear delineation to be made between the adult part of her personality and infantile structures. These latter included a very dependent baby, urgently needing the 'toilet-mummy' (Meltzer, 1967) but afraid of falling from the height of the feeding-breast; and in addition there appeared a know-it-all big sister part. This was the part that knew better than mummy and sat in harsh judgement on almost everyone. The one exception to this was seen to be her maternal grandmother, to whom the qualities of 'parental' continued to have adhered historically. This was paralleled in the analysis by the status of Melanie Klein, while the analyst, like the parents, was felt to be highly sexual but of dubious reliability.

As we proceeded into the third year of the analysis Mrs D. seemed to lapse into a desultory type of resistance to the work, bringing her material with a shrug and listening to interpretations with scarcely disguised boredom and misgivings about what seemed to her the analyst's cavalier attitude towards evidence. She explicitly considered as unworthy of respect a so-called science whose criteria of truth-function lay in the aesthetic realm, which proved nothing and could convince no one. This reached hilarious proportions one day in an incident involving a cobweb hanging from the ceiling of the consulting room. Somehow the question arose as to its origin; did it necessarily imply a spider or were other events possible, such as particles of dust adhering by static electricity. Mrs D. promptly looked it up, not in a physics or biology text but in the *New Oxford Dictionary*, and that was that. The possibility of my personal experience was ruled out in favour of definition. Whatever the analyst's experience of other phenomena might have been, they could not have been 'cobwebs'. He was making a linguistic error, playing the wrong 'language-game' (Wittgenstein, 1953).

This debate about meaning and its relation to language came as climax to a series of dreams involving the patient's mother. Frequently the two of them were climbing hills together, having picnics on cliffs overlooking the sea or were upstairs in a house preparing food. In these many settings she was in continual conflict with her mother as to whose judgement was best. Her mother was endlessly patient, yielding and kind while she was endlessly tolerant of mother's limited knowledge, her rigidity, her age and fatigue, provincial narrowness, etc. The problem of bringing this baby

81

into a trusting dependence on the breast was clearly aggravated by the persistence of her infantile identity being invested in the 'big sister' part. It seemed quite hopeless as she lay session after session treating the analytical method in this way, bored, playing with her beads, shrugging her baby-shoulders, marching off at the end of the session with her baby-nose in the air. But a dream gave promise of a chink in the armour.

Two months earlier she had had a dream which seemed to make reference to her dislike of the timbre of her own voice: *she discovered that the piano sounded so poorly because there was a weasel hiding in it and producing a corrosive froth. But when she tried to put it out the window, it kept getting back inside despite the two big guard-dogs.* This seemed to link clearly with the acid contempt in her voice, with her eyes always ferreting out the defects and overlooking the virtues of the analyst. The way in which this operated to frustrate the breast in its attempts to fill the baby with something good and the way it was related to the perverse sexual trends found a brilliantly condensed representation in a very frightening and crucial dream with a rich associative framework. In the dream *it seemed that scripture was no longer to be taught in the schools in London as the children would not accept it unless it was called something high-flown like 'moral philosophy'. Then she seemed to be in a classroom where one girl was passing out pieces of cotton wool while another was making a mystic invocation to invite a giant bird to swoop down and carry off some other girl. At that moment a bird-woman appeared at the window, beating against the glass with her wings and a piece of wood. Mrs D. felt terrified she would break in.*

The associations to the dream were revealing and poignant. When they had been in Canada, living in a cottage, a robin had come every morning and beat against the bedroom window. Mrs D. thought it must have had a nest there when the cottage had stood unoccupied. On the day before the dream the patient had had to go to Oxford on business and had felt uneasy that she might see the analyst on the street there. But instead, to her dismay, on the way home she had seen her mother get off to change trains at Reading. She did not see or hear the patient call to her because Mrs D. could not open the window. She realized that she could have had the pleasure of riding with her mother had not her omniscience prevented her phoning the cousin with whom mother was staying in Oxford, so certain had she been that mother's visit was to last longer.

It was unmistakable, therefore, that the bird-woman in the dream, like the robin in Canada, represented her mother trying to get back in touch with the good baby, who, however, was being made deaf to the truth (the cotton for the ears?) and dominated by the propaganda of the know-it-all seance-holding weasel-eyed 'big sister'. Theoretically this would represent an inability to effect a satisfactory splitting-and-idealization of self and object (Klein, 1932).

In the months that followed an interesting and very gradual alteration in behaviour and mood took place in the consulting room. The shoulder-shrugging contempt for the psychoanalytical method and the spiteful scepticism about its efficacy, all based on her delusion-of-clarity-of-insight and sitting-in-judgement, changed to a brooding pessimism about herself and her character. She felt keenly the adamantine streak in herself and how it resisted being helped or being dependent, how it clung somehow by preference to the promise of perverse excitement, even though it no longer put this into action. She began to note similar qualities among some of the people she had previously admired and to see how it wrecked their constructive aims and cost so much pain to the people who were fond of them. It was at first a harsh judgement on herself, one that would have passed sentence for punishment, but slowly this softened to sympathy and regret, even at times a bit remorseful, for the pain she inflicted on others and on herself. She felt herself to be a real 'schizophrenogenic' mother and wondered at the flourishing of her children, who indeed did seem somehow to have benefited more from her analysis than she had herself. It was striking now how session after session she arrived in gloom and left cheerful. She insisted that this was just because I let her talk about her children and that was nice. Still she could recognize that the cheerfulness had something to do with the analyst's 'foolish optimism' getting into her temporarily. She even was beginning to think there might be a beauty in the method that she could not see. But mainly her good feelings adhered to the analyst very personally. It was he who could bear the weasel-eyes and the shoulder-shrugging. Perhaps someday she would shed the secrecy about her love and wear her heart on her sleeve. But it would have to be very slow; she was not a plunger-in.

Almost on the anniversary of the 'bird-woman' dream another amused Mrs D. and heartened the analyst, for in it *a young lion was hurling himself at her windscreen and it seemed only a matter of time before he broke through. But later she was outside the car lifting a cat in her arms and closing some gate to keep a child from straying out of the garden.* It was quite clear to her now that the delusion-of-clarity-of-insight came from being inside her object looking out its eyes and that the world, and the analysis, looked quite different from outside. The frightening lion-breast, like the bird-woman, became the attractive cat-breast that she could now take into herself as the basis of her own motherliness.

SUMMARY

This short paper on the psychopathology of insight and judgement has set out to demonstrate one type of disturbance which can be seen to arise from the operation of the unconscious infantile phantasy of projective identification with the internal objects, especially the mother's breast and head, experienced as the font of knowledge and wisdom. Fragments of material have been brought to illustrate the operation of the mechanism and then a more extensive description of an analysis was attempted. This latter sought to trace the relation of the patient's character pathology to a defensive structure which had been mounted in the second year of life under the pressure of disappointment and jealousy of the new baby sister. While in many ways the harshness and judgemental quality of the character was in the nature of a revenge against the parents for expelling her from a blissful confusion of identity with them, it was also a defence against ever being caught so unawares again. Thus her epistemophilic instinct and high intelligence were re-enforced by defensive as well as aggressive motives. In the transference it was necessary to work through the dissolution of the narcissistic organization illustrated best in the 'bird-woman' dream. In order to do this a difficult countertransference problem of tolerating hopelessness and humiliation had to be faced, throwing light on the magnitude of the difficulties from which Mrs D.'s parents had retreated. It is difficult to see how parents, no matter how sterling, could have done otherwise.

The internal experience of these two mental acts, delusion-of-clarity-of-insight and sitting-in-judgement, seems to shade so subtly into their healthy counterparts, insight and judgement, that it is difficult to see how anything other than a widening of the field of introspection could distinguish 'them. Respect for the laws of evidence, attention to the quality of reasoning, soliciting the opinion of others in crucial matters and other safeguards may help. But such intellectual and social safety-measures also pay a price by throwing away the possible moment of inspiration that seems to have no evidential links, to which the laws of logic find no application and which may seem unintelligible when communicated to others for advice. And since all nascent creativity may be based on the seizing of such moments, Kierkegaard's (1941) 'leap in the dark', there comes a time when reliance on one's own introspection, forlornly, must be attempted.

REFERENCES

BREUER, J. & FREUD, S. (1893 – 1895). Studies on hysteria. *S. E.* **2.**
FREUD, S. (1918). From the history of an infantile neurosis. *S. E.* **17.**
KIERKEGAARD S. (1941). *Fear and Trembling.* Princeton: Princeton Univ. Press.
KLEIN, M. (1932). *The Psycho-Analysis of Children.* London: Hogarth Press.
KLEIN, M. (1946). Notes on some schizoid mechanisms. In *Developments in Psycho-Analysis.* London: Hogarth Press, 1952.
MELTZER, D. (1967). *The Psycho-Analytical Process.* London: Heinemann.
WITTGENSTEIN, L. (1953). *Philosophical Investigations.* Oxford: Blackwell.

This description, which probably covers the category of pseudo-maturity, applies mainly to people whose entry to the claustrum was sealed in the latency period, when its identificatory aspects were in so many ways adaptive to school and parental requirement. But the disturbances of personality which are built around the life experience in the claustrum and profoundly colour the person's view-of-the-world seem to have earlier, pregenital origins but burst forth in puberty. From the Proustian world we move to the world of Gonchorov's *Oblomov* and Melville's *Bartleby*.

Here we find the big, indolent baby boys and the doll's-house little girls, for whom the supreme value is comfort. They are voluptuous without eroticism, curious without interest, obedient from inertia and polite without consideration. What they enjoy seems to them what the whole world is striving for, an eternal holiday with companionship but without relationship, in a pretty world without disturbing aesthetic impact. If they have money or an effortless means of earning it, they are content, but their ideal is to be pampered without any recrimination for parasitism. They can meet sexual demands in a passive and voluptuous way, and find social acceptance by their bland enjoyment of everything. Addictions do not ensnare them nor hypochondria trouble them, so long as they are comfortable. Other people like them, tolerate their uselessness and are pleased to indulge them, "for it gives them such pleasure". They hardly notice the passage of time and the ageing process, and usually remain fresh and juvenile looking. Neat without being fastidious, clean without being obsessional, they find the operations of bathing, dressing and grooming pleasing and enjoyably time consuming. Other people's way of life seems to them frantic, purposeless and deeply unnecessary. But they view themselves as tolerant, minding their own business, which does not include any obligation to be of use in the world, for the world seems to them blessedly self-sustaining. Pleasant zephyrs of ambition blow through them from time to time, to write, or paint or travel, "when they have time". As their sexuality is largely pregenital and undifferentiated, and since they are most content being kept as pets, they often have an opportunistically ambisexual history. They can even accommodate perversion, but without enthusiasm. Their ideal is a pseudo-intimacy of outward affection and tolerance screening the quid pro quo taking turns at serving one another. One is inclined to tiptoe away from encounters with such couples thinking wryly, "That's nice, children. Don't fight". If the affection such people arouse does not come through from this acid description, perhaps a little joke will make the point:

> Mother (on the telephone): yes, darling, of course I'll come over — yes, and bring some corn flakes and milk for the children — yes, I can bring my hoover with me — I can collect the repair man on the way — I'll take the car to be serviced — of course I'll shovel the snow from the drive first. It's Saturday. Why doesn't Paul do it — what do you mean, who's Paul? Your husband — What? Harry! What number is this? — You're not my daughter!
>
> Daughter: Does that mean you're not coming?

For such indolent baby boys and girls, however, every wind is a hurricane. If she loses her purse, poverty stares her in the face. If he has indigestion after a big meal, cancer looms. Every separation is a desertion, every cross word is the end of the affair. "Shouldn't you get a job?" is a great betrayal and laughter at the next table means her shoes don't match her skirt. But being masters of scotomization, they hardly notice anything that would disturb their complacency.

In personalities where the sense of identity is dominated by an infantile part intrusively ensconced in the head/breast, the two states of Proustian and Oblomovian view-of-the-world are often seen to oscillate and may even give an impression of a cyclothymic instability. But this is misleading, for the cyclothyme alternates between being overpowered by an intrusive identification with a gravely damaged object and then escaping. His grandiosity is hidden in his depression, while the mania celebrates his liberation, a fiesta of self-indulgence and vitality.

The compartmentalized view-of-the-world seems always to produce an obsessive interest in the other compartments and its inhabitants. The dwellers of the head/breast are, by and large, disdainful of the sex-obsessed ones in the genital space and the dirty rascals in the rectum.

LIFE IN THE GENITAL COMPARTMENT

The inmates of this space are more obviously disturbed and turbulent than those of the head/breast, for they live in a space that is dominated by a primitive priapic religion. So close is its resemblance to the adolescent community that some pains must be taken to make the distinction. The adolescent is more like the manic-depressive in configuration, when home has taken on a claustrophobic atmosphere and the parents have become "old", meaning debilitated, seized-up, sexless. The escape from home releases great vitality based on great expectations and an overestimation of intelligence, knowledge and potency. The community of adolescents is, of course, obsessed with sex, both pre-genital greed and genital longings, but it is not a primitive religion, more like a political party seeking a leader.

This adolescent community gives cover to the inhabitants of all three interior compartments through its hedonism and ever-shifting fashions, but they are detectable by their extremity, by "over-the-top" qualities. When we meet genital dwellers who are still children we always suspect that they have been used, if not abused, by grown-ups or older children. And this is almost a certainty, for so powerful is the seductiveness of the erotic state of mind and its priapic preoccupation that sexual encounters with bigger persons is almost inevitable. They have known no latency period and tend to be shunned by other children unless their charisma enables them to form a gang, a local "fuck club". But generally in this age group they are somewhat isolated and have a masturbation chamber, a "tree-house" at home or the lavatory at school. The boys are the grafitti artists who festoon public lavatories with representations of genitals, while the girls are readers of romance and endless drawers of fashionable princesses with long hair and big eyes.

In this group the identificatory aspect is flamboyant in its macho maleness and coquettish femininity, for they treat their bodies as decorations of the soul to be ever more decorated and beautified. This preoccupation stems from the qualities of the priapic religion which has an absolute belief in the "irresistible" object and animal magnetism. Whether the burning desire is to *be* the irresistible phallus or to have absolute power over it, the essential object is the erect penis. All this is freely displayed and in the adolescent community passes undetected as a disturbance, for the "over-the-top" ones are not shunned as in latency but admired. But the anxieties generated by the claustrophobic intrusive phantasy in the form of fears of disease and pregnancy prevents concentration on studies, interferes with sleep and sets up all manner of feeding irregularities and obsessions.

Any understanding of this priapic religion must come from a view of the unconscious masturbation phantasies, for the conscious ones are utterly banal and pornographic. To understand the qualities of this interior compartment as seen from the inside, we must contrast it with the unconscious image of the mother's genital and her relationship to the father and his genital as construed from actual observation and relationship to the parents. In psychic reality the parental bedroom is a sanctum of mysterious and revered rites in which the father, with his penis and his semen nourishes, fertilizes and cleanses the mother's procreative organs through all three of her major orifices. She is full of babies. Love and work here reach their culminating integration.

Seen from the interior through the eyes of the intruder, it is Mardi Gras, a festival of priapic religion where the beauty of femininity has the irresistible power to produce the erection that is irresistibly fascinating and craved by every sense and orifice. Titian's "Offering to Venus" (Prado) showing her statue in a landscape of putti, Bosch's "Garden of Earthly Pleasures" (Prado) depict its pagan atmosphere. For the essence of this interior view is that the entry of the father's phallus is celebrated and enjoyed voluptuously by all the babies, while the mother calmly receives this homage. Central to the erotic charge is the disproportion between the smallness of the children and the bigness of the phallus. To enjoy this phantasy the girl must be petite, relatively unformed, with small breasts. The boy, in his masculine projective identification with this phallus must be big, muscular, powerful. Dissatisfaction with the size of his penis is of little account, for his whole body is phallus. The libretto of intrusion that accompanies the music of the adolescent community, constant and enveloping, is a simple one. The father's phallus enters in order to be entertained and worshipped in Dionysiac fashion to the point of exhaustion after the fireworks of ejaculation. The pleasure is mutual, of worshipper and worshipped and only a thin partition separates it from sado-masochism and degradation. For the girl there is the additional pleasure of a secret oedipal triumph: daddy's erection is not a response to mother's beauty but an expectation of encountering her with her nubile prettiness inside. For the boy the oedipal conflict is by-passed in favour of being worshipped by a seraglio of little girls to whom he is master. The disproportion in size plus the strong pregenital orientation favours kissing, sucking and masturbating the phallus rather than genital intercourse.

For the adolescent community the bacchanale and orgy may be represented at discos, pop concerts and parties, but its actual devolution into group sex belongs to the erotomanic or the perverse. Such distinctions highlight the failure of symbol formation in the interior world. The phallus *as* fetish is a far cry from fetishism. While the feverish aspects of the sexual cravings of the genital cave-dweller do not bring him disapprobation but rather admiration from peers, he cannot escape the lingering sense of being an interloper amidst the joyousness of adolescent eroticism. Not only does he feel in imminent danger of being seduced over the border into perversity, but the need for multiple, transient and swift encounters makes a link with the essential feeling of treachery for the girl, in her secret oedipal triumph over a casual lover's wife; but feelings of cowardice for the boy in his evasion of competition, essentially oedipal, for his eye is always on the alert for the easy target and stereotyped sexiness. The consequence is the formation, analogous to the perverse subcommunity, of an erotomanic subcommunity of adolescents, stretching well into the thirties. By astute selection of targets for seduction and decisive sexual moves, they both, male and female, arrange a satisfying confirmation of their phantasy of irresistibility. Is this eponymously the world of Goethe, for which Kierkegaard and later Mann so envied and despised him?

LIFE IN THE MATERNAL RECTUM

We arrive finally at the heart of this book, at the area of intrusive identification which contains the greatest potentiality for serious mental disturbance. It might be said that the foregoing description of life in the head/breast and genital produce a variety of rigid and restricted immaturity, not incompatible with adaptation to the requirements of casual/contractual aspects of community life, though quite prejudicial to the establishment of intimate/family relationships. But there is a perilously slippery chute from head to rectum as voluptuousness leads to eroticism and on to sado-masochism.

In essence we are dealing with the region of psychic reality where the atmosphere of sadism is pervasive and the hierarchic structure of tyranny and submission forebodes violence. For this reason, unlike the other two compartments where comfort and erotic pleasure dominate the value system, in the rectal compartment there is only one value: survival. Although the sadism may vary in intensity as one moves along the spectrum from boarding school to concentration camp, the atmosphere of incipient terror is probably little changed, for one meets evidence that the nameless dread consists in being "thrown away". This will be expanded in the chapter on the onset of schizophrenia, but it is worthwhile to keep in mind that this nameless dread is exponentially worse even than exile and Cain's lament: it is absolute loneliness in a world of bizarre objects.

Seen from the outside of the object, the rectum of the internal mother is construed as the storehouse of the debris engendered by the internal and external babies who cannot refrain from fouling the nest, either for themselves or for the others. The internal father and his genital are assumed to perform heroic tasks of a life-saving nature for the mother and her brood. The concept of the heroic in masculinity and male sexuality probably has its roots here and plays such a large part in the erotic concepts and behaviour of the adolescent community.

But seen from the inside, intruded into by stealth or violence in anal masturbation or anal assault, it is a region of satanic religion, ruled by the great fecal penis, the world of Orwell's "Big Brother". It is thus a world of groups, or rather tribes, of

91

Bion's Basic Assumption Groups; a world of assumption rather than thought, where right means either the law or precedent, where to be genuinely different means to be detected as an intruder by the great "Jew Detector". The prisoners of this system, where the term claustrophobia takes on its most poignant significance, have only two choices: outward conformity or joining as lieutenants of the great leader, the fecal penis.

One way or another, the outcome is degradation, not only, of course, in behaviour, but more essentially — being less equivocal — in concepts and the ability to think as a basis for action. Truth is transformed into anything that cannot be disproved; justice becomes talion plus an increment; all the acts of intimacy change their meaning into techniques of manipulation or dissimulation; loyalty replaces devotion; obedience substitutes for trust; emotion is simulated by excitement; guilt and the yearning for punishment takes the place of regret. Bion's conclusion that the natural leader of the Basic Assumption Group is a schizoid psychopath seems absolutely true, and the route of degradation induced by the continual recruitment to lieutenancy leads in this direction. But the degradation of ethics must have already reached fundamentals before the prisoner is ready to don the uniform and degrade another ("don't do it to me; do it to him/her"). The idea of fear of death has lost its descriptive power in this situation. In fact death is longed for and suicidal ruminations hover in the background continually. It is of interest to note that serious but unsuccessful suicidal attempts not infrequently produce release from this claustrum and take on the flavour of religious conversion.

Facts of this sort remind one that we are essentially in the world of addiction, where the individual has consigned his survival to the mercy of a malignant object. In fact the great fecal penis is not an object, but a self object, compounded of a bad (disappointing, deserting) object and a cold (minus LHK) part of the self at part object level, therefore primitive. This view has profound significance for our idea of the human condition, for it eliminates evil as an intrinsic concept and reduces it to a behavioural, descriptive one. This opens a vista on the therapeutic possibilities, for this great malignant object is potentially metabolizable into its component parts of self and object, dissolving the malignant character of the combination. But the therapeutic task is a difficult one, for this compounded object is a master of confusion and cynicism, appropriating to itself the quality of the internal father, of heroism and protectiveness. The heroism is of particular interest, for it alleges to be a hero-of-the-resistance to the tyranny of ethical considerations, by definition, the crucial one going far beyond the ego-centricity of the paranoid-schizoid position. Its claim is a cynical one: any curb placed upon a desire out of consideration for the opinions, feelings or well-being of another is slavery. The sanctimony with which this can be announced is breath-taking.

Although the mental state is essentially an imprisonment and scintillating with claustrophobia, it is not necessarily devoid of pleasures and satisfactions, setting aside the dubiously erotic ones of the sexual perversions, the drug addict's trips, the criminal's triumphs. In analysis one meets a strange type of self-idealization which also claims to be hero-of-the-resistance, but this time of resistance to the tyrannical system itself. It is essentially the game of double agent. While you appear to be satisfying the requirements of lieutenancy by appearing to degrade others, in fact you are teaching them the evils of the system and — by graded lessons — fostering their resistance to the pressure of the recruitment if they are already inmates of the claustrum, or warning the outsiders against the temptation to enter. It is frighteningly modelled, through cynicism, on the psycho-analytical method and parental care. Only the dreams of frank cruelty to children break through the web of devious language usage, at which they are masters, for they can hardly talk without rehearsal nor come to a session without an agenda. We will discuss the difficulties of the countertransference in the chapter on technical problems.

This aspect of the mental state, the self-idealization, is quite different from grandiosity, of which one meets two different sorts. Of course those who are recruited to lieutenancy experience an intense grandiosity through the identificatory aspect of life within the object, both with the maternal object who welcomes the fecal penis and participates masochistically in the atrocities, and with the fecal penis that rules this underworld. But another type of grandiosity can be observed that appears to be an inversion of the sense of being an intruder, namely a sense of being different from all the other inhabitants, the exception. This status is preserved by a kind of colourlessness, of social invisibility, in which minimal conformity is accompanied by aloofness from the excitement. This fly-on-the-wall technique results in an attitude of being in the audience to life's horrific dramas yet it cannot escape the excitation of the voyeur.

Those fallen angels who have yielded to the recruitment are the ones who suffer most while most frantically seeking relief from the despair. They are the most dogged by suicidal ruminations, the most accident prone, the ones who expose themselves to violence and punishment. At the same time, because their world is not only compartmentalized but absolutely hierarchic, they manifest what can only be called a frantic ambitiousness. The concept of "the top" is very concrete for them and has the meaning of security, albeit they know very well how uneasy rests the head that wears the crown. For this reason they are essentially political in their orientation and ruthless in their conniving for power in whatever field they dwell, big or small, it makes no difference. As life is felt to be essentially institutional, "the top" is "The top" wherever. "Caesar or nothing".

It is an unfortunate fact that these recruits do come to analysis, driven by despair, bad dreams, insomnia, exhaustion. But they do not come for the purpose of struggling against their essential imprisonment but only against the emotional consequences, their "symptoms", often psychosomatic. Where their frantic ambitiousness does not sufficiently express their imprisonment but is supplemented by perversity or criminality, one often finds that all their powers of dissimulation have been expended to construct a completely respectable facade in their social life: spouse, children, civic activities, insurance policies, punctilious dress and behaviour, all as a screen for both the perversity and the despair. It is no wonder that the posh hotels have windows that only open a few inches. It is worth noting in passing how different is this frantic ambitiousness of the rectum-dwellers from the scrambling after fame and rather messianic ambitiousness of the head/breast inhabitant.

One of the puzzling features of this population, which one

notices quite strongly in the analytic situation, is that they are frightening. They need not be big men. Quite small and frail-looking women can have it but it is difficult to simulate. How difficult for an actress to be a convincing Lady Macbeth. No, it is a mysterious charisma that paralyzes the opposition. Somehow they are able to produce an atmosphere of hostage-holding, even if one cannot quite detect the identity of the hostage. It is always one's loved ones, in the last resort the children.

6   Technical Problems of the Claustrum

In previous chapters the centre of interest has been on the personalities in whom the sense of identity has become fixed in that infantile part which is an inhabitant of the claustrum. And it is with this population that the special technical problems arise. In the normal and neurotic person, the entry into analysis ,may, and usually does, commence with a preformed trans-'ference which has gathered its expectations from literature, films, friends' accounts. It is generally either austerely institutional or wildly romantic and is set aside fairly promptly when the setting has been clarified, the method outlined, cooperation requested, the first dreams are interpreted, and the week-end breaks begin to have an impact. The need for objects of infantile transference then favours the gradual attraction of these facets of the personality into the ambience of the analysis, the "gathering of the transference". Experience strongly suggests that the most satisfactory answer to the question "why do you seek analysis?" would be, "Because I need to gather together my needs for infantile transference so that there may be some possibility of working conflicts through instead of repeatedly enacting them." Perhaps it will be thought that I am using transference in a restricted sense when I stress both "infantile" and need of an "object", but it is my understanding of the term that transference derives from the externalization of the relationship to internal objects, and has therefore the configuration of family life. It stands in continual oscillation with the organization of narcissism, that is, those activities and alliances of infantile structures which are outside the direct influence of the parental figures and usually in opposition to their values.

The pre-formed transference with people who seek re-analysis because of an impasse in previous attempts is quite different, and takes a long time to be set aside completely. It is based on the "particularities" of the previous analyst, as Freud would say, which seemed to give such concrete reality to the transference that it could not be resolved. This may or may not involve situations where the essential aspects of setting and communication have been lost sight of in the hubbub of the emotionality on both sides.

What I am about to describe of the technical problems with people whose *sense of identity* is fixed in the interior world is based so absolutely on the countertransference that, except for exemplification in dreams, one would have to consider it entirely in the imagination of the therapist. For this reason what follows will either resonate with the reader's clinical experience as patient and therapist, or it will seem a fairy story. It can hardly be exemplified in work with adult patients and perhaps much of the conviction behind this description comes from work with children. My previous writings, from the *Psycho-analytical Process* on, are full of examples and I will not attempt to repeat it here, since either a therapist has treated children and seen it, or has not, and descriptions do not speak to him.

Instead of exemplification, the attempt will be made to cull out the special qualities of the analytic interaction and to describe them in an evocative way. The qualities of the phantasy life have already been described for all three compartments, and it has been acknowledged that the difficulty of synthesis in the analyst's mind is somewhat due to a certain mobility from one compartment to another. The severity of the disturbance in the personality is more determined by the rigidity than by the degree of immaturity of the ensconsed part, if one measures severity in terms of incapacity for intimate emotional relationships, and therefore of potential for analytic therapy. Thus the pseudo-mature personality may prove far more fixed and resistant to change than, say, an adolescent whose hold on reality seems precarious. The reasons for this will be explored. But in analysis the proof-of-the-pudding has the final say, and every failure has to be assumed to be laid at the door of the analyst and our still — after a century — immature science.

It does not seem useful to spend any time discussing the "reasons" that bring such patients to analysis. Like anyone else, they come voluntarily, and/or are sent; they come because of vague or tormenting distress, because of curiosity, idleness, daring, trouble making, defiance. It makes little difference after the first few sessions. But what characterizes them all is the rigidity of the preformed transference which emanates from their view-of-the-world. It is this that we must try to evoke.

Often the first thing that strikes the therapist is the surprising appearance of cooperation in the method as outlined, for it is so different from what was expected on the basis of the suspiciousness the patients manifest in the consultation, the tentativeness with which the offer of an attempt at analysis was accepted, the restrictions placed on the frequency of sessions, pleading limited time, money, the distance of travel and other logistics. But it is not long before the shallowness and docility of the cooperation makes itself apparent. One senses that they bring material, largely anecdotal and anamnestic, which they think interests analysts. The emotionality has been sifted from the voice and the vocabulary is characterized by a near virtuosity in ambiguity. The analyst finds that he is left with no vivid visual image of the events or persons, that names are often replaced with titles of relationship, so that one becomes confused about the personae, the locus, the time sequences. Consequently it becomes necessary to seek continual clarification, which the patient greets with a suppressed irritability. Is one in the presence of thought disorder? Is it all true or confabulated for your delectation or titillation? Who are you supposed to be that this person is willing to come, lie on your couch and talk away?

Correspondingly, if one treats this material in the ordinary way, attempts to formulate or to relate external events to the immediacy of the supposed transference, one is thrown back by an encounter with a jarring rubberiness which appears to be a mixture of tolerance, inattention and contempt, "I knew you would say that" remaining unspoken — temporarily. The subsequent material moves on in a clearly pre-programmed way, whether the patient has politely paused to let you do your stuff, or you have had to elbow your way into the monologue. Soon, from dropped items like, "I was thinking in the car coming", it becomes clear that an agenda is in progress of unfolding. But it is worse than that, as the music of insincerity begins to be tuned into. This takes time because such people have spent long years practising dissimulation on exactly this topic in order to hide from themselves and others their trespasser status.

If, despite the patient's somewhat intimidating rattle of incipient irritability, the analyst persists in trying to define the factual data the patient is alleging to convey — what actually was done, said, seen, heard — the impression develops that one is hearing a journalistic account rather than a report of an emotional experience. The events of childhood are of particular interest, for one finds that the patient cannot at all distinguish between memory and hearsay, whether the account has come from others, like family folk-lore, or from himself, the story he made up at the time to tell his friends, or from his diary or internal dossier of grievances. The impression persists that the patient is not remembering an event but recalling an account of an event, an account of very dubious validity.

Equally disquieting is the impersonality of the patient's entry and exit. Either he does not look in one's eyes or has the terrible capacity to look through you or just past your ear. Similarly he seems to take the room, its furnishing, the mode of entry, the qualities of the couch, etc. for granted, of no interest. But this is belied by the frequency with which one can note items of the ambience appearing in the dreams, which, when pointed out, the patient denies ever having noticed. And it is true, he has seen but not noticed, not only the room and its furnishings, but you — your age, baldness, whether you wear spectacles, have a beard, dress elegantly or like a tramp, are fat or thin, tall or short, attractive or repulsive. But if the analyst changes jacket or dress, the colour change may appear in the patient's costume the next day. Any attempt to investigate this makes the rattle of irritability decibels louder. But this is generally true of any suggestion of the unconscious being operative, for after all, what more complete denial of psychic reality can there be than to be living inside it.

Finally the penny drops: you are not an individual but a representative of a particular institution called psycho-analysis, with its hierarchy and its Kafkaesque mysteries. Once this becomes apparent, you sense that the ordinary procedure of psycho-analysis, based on the culling out and description of the transference, is hardly in order, for there is no infantile transference in this ordinary sense. Instead the consulting room is a particular cubicle in a particular institution in an institutionalized world. Or you may gradually discover that it is a particular cubicle in one of three compartments in a particular institution of an institutionalized world and that the other two are elsewhere. You may notice that your cubicle is a torture chamber, or hothouse of eroticism or a place of heavenly peace and rest. But it is nonetheless part of an institution and you are on the staff. Just what is your status in the hierarchy may become a matter of great interest and concern. But this is not infantile transference, despite evidence of fascination.

All of this does in fact bind the patient to the analysis and in a sense it does "gather" some of the processes of his infantile life in a way that has a clarifying, ameliorative effect on other relationships and activities. It may seem to function as·infantile transference of the toilet-breast variety, but it lacks urgency, relief, pleasure and the evacuation of anxieties. Consequently the countertransference remains somewhat fallow, one feels existent but unused despite analytic efforts. Or perhaps because of analytic efforts which meet no evident reception, evoke no evident reverberations of emotion.

But while one garners suggestions of improvement in the patient's life outside analysis — mainly by negative evidence, in fact, and this seems to explain the attachment to the procedure — very positive evidence that the patient is becoming "worse" in his mental state is not spared you. Transference neurosis? I am afraid not. Merely a widening of the patient's consciousness due to the analyst's persistent efforts to improve observation and clarify communication. This latter, which has both lexical and conceptual aspects, is a particular annoyance to the patient, for he is far more interested in a Thesaurus view of language, where apparent synonyms are easily interchangeable, than a dictionary where usages are particular and synonyms cease to exist. New concepts, on the other hand, since they require efforts of imagination, pass him by and are treated as jargon of your institution.

Taking all this into account, I think that interpreting the transference has a negative effect, for it presents the patient not only with the anathema of the unconscious but also seems to him an insistence by the analyst on intimacy and dependence. Being totally unaware of such sentiments he can only conclude that the analyst's behaviour is either doctrinaire or a manifestation of his loneliness and isolation, cooped up all day in his drab consulting room, tending one stranger after another by means of a dubious method, a fate softened only by the amount of money he is able to harvest.

This view of the analyst, of which one gets hints at moments of extreme irritation in the patient, hints which slip out and are quickly denied, declare the position precisely. Unlike the neurotic patient, who at the height of oedipal feelings will rail at the analyst as exercising droit de seigneur, being autocratic, living a privileged life, the attitude of the inmate of the interior world is essentially contemptuous. For it is based on the unchallenged assumption that this interior world is all there is and that the analyst is as much caught up in its net as is the patient but for some reason, some special psycho-analytical elitism, thinks himself above or beyond it all. He can detect in the analyst evidences of the stigmata of all three compartments, elitist parasitism, erotic pre-occupation and certainly sadism, hopefully masochism.

This irritability and covert contempt is catching. Nothing is easier than for such an attempt at analysis to resemble negative transference and countertransference while simply being an expression of two institutional co-workers increasingly disliking one another but feeling bound together by the task. From the patient's point of view it is a purely contractual relationship and it is the task of the analyst to make an analysis of this exercise. He cannot do it if he cannot find the child in the patient, for the carapace resists intimacy as terra incognita, a poetic myth, a denial of the essentially solipsistic nature of the human condition.

This imaginary world of the inside of an internal object — and after all it is all pure imagination which has borrowed forms from the outside world as its furniture but is based on nothing but the omnipotence of masturbation processes — evoked by an act of imaginative conjecture by the analyst, enables him to adopt a firm position outside the patient's world while paying him a friendly and concerned visit in the sessions. It is a surprisingly powerful position in its resistance to the irritant effect of the patient's secretiveness, insincerity and covert contempt. Above all it forestalls moral judgment, for it is a view that makes it apparent that the *person on your couch is an absolute stranger who is not displaying his personality but only his techniques of adaptation to the claustrophobic world he inhabits.* The moment an analyst can recognize the incarcerated quality and the essential struggle for survival in an unlivable situation, he sees a child who has lost his way, strayed from home, who has even forgotten the qualities of the home he once knew, perhaps in the most severe cases only the womb.

Experience eventually adds another dimension to this concerned tolerance, for it demonstrates that the claustrum is in fact not a closed space like the delusional system, not is it, albeit imaginary in its qualities, cut off from psychic reality and therefore from the outside world. Even before clinical experience has enabled this suspicion to ripen into conviction, the recognition of such a possibility enables the analyst to recognize what one might call the negative aspects of the claustrum, namely what experiential areas it is cut off from, be the door ever so open. This has already been mentioned but perhaps would bear some enlargement at this point since it is vital to the analyst's demonstrations to the patient of the nature of the world he is living in.

The patient's dreams are forever declaring this problem: he is looking out the window, talking to someone through the window of a departing train, in an airport terminal where he knows no one, in the audience, looking down at the activities of others, in company where a foreign language is being spoken, etc. The essential fact is that human relationships and the world in its natural or manmade aspects make no emotional impact, except for the distant thunder of anxiety. He is continually having to construct a story of emotional impact, based on hearsay and fading recollection, which at best can induce a state of excitement simulating feelings. He can "make himself" laugh, cry, be sexually aroused, cozy, horrified, vengeful — the whole range of emotions, but without authenticity, conviction. When he displays these induced states he feels furtive, fraudulent. He cannot consequently experience any belief in the authenticity of the words, music or display of feelings by others. The suffering from this state would be continual were it not for the development of powers of scotomization and a cynical assumption that it is the same for all, a sham.

When the analyst can see, with his imaginative eye, this predicament and recognize — through the gloss of sophistication and banality — the lost child, patience and tolerance become vibrant in him and are reflected in his words, the music of his voice, the look in his eye, if only the patient could notice such aspects. Where such an insight by the analyst is very conscious and formulated as it is here, the patience and tolerance enable him to persevere, hold the patient to him despite the mounting storm of holiday breaks. The optimism about slow and steady progress which was expressed in Chapter II of *The Psycho-analytical Process* seems still correct. But the pitfalls of routine psycho-analytical work are equally clear. The mounting dislike and mutual irritability either produce an explosive interruption on one part or the other, or the patient tip-toes away on logistic grounds, generally a geographic change engineered quietly. But a modus vivendi may be worked out by mutual accommodation, ending, when the patient reports sufficient improvement in his external adaptation, in a sort of mutual idealization, each awarding the other the Good Housekeeping Seal of Approval. At worst they may settle into an interminable perversion of analysis.

Leaving out the area of work with schizophrenic patients, which seems to be pure heroism, the patients here discussed could be said to try analysts' souls. Is it any wonder that Bion admonishes us to make the best of a bad job, when one can never be sure which path one is following, which outcome has ensued! In my experience, as the method I am outlining has become more clearly defined and more consistently put into practice, the danger of mutual adaptation and idealization, of seduction by external improvements in socialization, is certainly obviated. For the patient gets "worse" and leaves no doubt about it in the analyst's mind. The danger of explosion on one side or the other is clearly lessened. But what takes their place is the growing conviction in the patient, and a parallel suspicion in the analyst, that the analysis is all rubbish, that the analyst is just as ensconced in his psycho-analytical claustrum as the patient, that it isn't even the *halt* leading the blind but a couple of blind philosophers mistaking an elephant's legs for a forest. One's negative capability is put to the test indeed!

For this aspect of what is really an attempt to make an analysis without the aid of a patient's need for transference objects is not a matter of weeks or months, but years. Mutual exhaustion threatens as things get "worse". The technical procedure, if it can be called that, required by this mode of imaginative conjecture is basically a simple one. The first requirement is for the analyst to recognize that he is not yet presiding over a psycho-analytical process. This, I think, needs also to be conveyed to a patient, but with adamantine hopefulness. Unfortunately this is extremely irritating to the patient, even though it also holds him to the task. In this atmosphere the analyst will find himself restricted to the role of a kind of tour guide around the claustrum, demonstrating from the patient's behaviour, his dreams and his anecdotal stories both the qualities of the interior world whose compartment he inhabits, his anxieties, manifest and incipient, and his modes of adaptation, in and out of the analytical room.

This method, which the patient experiences as relentless and sadistic, spoiling and envious, has two directions and two consequences. First of all it is aimed at undoing the areas of self-idealization by investigating the story-making, the cynical attitudes towards others, especially the analyst, and the spuriousness of the pleasures of indolence, elitism, erotomania or the hero-of-the resistance. Correspondingly this activity of the analyst widens the patient's awareness of the claustrophobic state, that he is in a state of mind that is not, in fact, universal and that he does not know how to get out of it. Those in the rectum, especially the double agents, begin to feel the nightmare quality of their lives and can no longer deny the dangers of the enactment of this state in their external world relationships and activities.

But there is a third consequence which comes only very slowly, the suspicion, growing to a conviction eventually (to the great relief of the analyst) that the therapist is not an inhabitant but only a visitor to the claustrum, a visitation which is not, by any means, devoid of the danger of becoming an inmate. One sees it too often in supervision to be able to remain with a sense of immunity to this industrial hazard. However, being whatever relief it is to the analyst, it greatly increases the patient's distress because, with the growth of conviction that the analyst is a visitor, the meaningfulness of the analytical breaks begins to belly out with the wind of envy. And with it the concept of family life starts to take on some substance beyond the boring, the contractual, the bourgeois, the timid, the safety net of respectability. By the time this has begun to happen and the patient has begun to notice the analyst as an individual, expressing his individual thought, feeling, imagination, the original motives for the intrusive identification begin to declare themselves. And with this the analyst's myth of masturbation and its noxious consequences begins to take on psychic reality.

At this point in the procedure an analytical process begins and the transference emerges from its hiding place, not only during the separations, that is in the absence of the object, but in its presence, as well, in the sessions. Acting in the transference begins to liven the deadliness of the patient's social adaptation, his emotional flatness, his obtuseness, his placatory docility, his unspoken contempt. Lightning attacks, frank flirtatiousness, demands for information and emotional directness spark the sessions. The patient's curiosity begins to monitor what is observable and scavengeable about the analyst's history and way of life. We are in business at last, on familiar territory of the transference-countertransference. The real life of the mind has entered the consulting room.

However, it is difficult at this point for the analyst to be at all certain what has happened, from a structural and geographic point of view. He cannot tell with any confidence whether the ensconced part of the personality has emerged from the claustrum or whether the sense of identity and therefore control of consciousness and behaviour has been wrested from it. The dreams are rather equivocal in this respect, because they tend in both cases to represent the infantile process of coming out, encountering mental pain, and hurrying back in again. The people in this category are unlike the normal and neurotic in whom an ensconced part has only been a complication, an impediment to their intimate lives. Because they have lived out fully their mental state in their view-of-the-world and adaptation to it, the reaction to emergence or shift of consciousness is still ambiguous. This seems to be because the reaction differs according to the compartment involved. Those who have been in the head/breast, both the Proustians and the Oblomovians, are assaulted by regret of the life-time they have wasted. The dwellers in the erotomanic compartment feel soiled and undesirable and feel a need for a purifying stay in the convent or monastery of abstinence, a kind of latency period. But those who have lived in the rectum are posed a severe depressive problem, for they may have done real damage in the world by enacting this state of mind.

Part 3

7   Emergence from the Claustrum versus Shift of Consciousness

It is a difficult problem to be able to state with any clarity what we mean by "understanding" in this science of psycho-analysis, but surely it has a dialectic. I am frequently reminded of the marvelous flight of imagination by Newton that produced the infinitesimal calculus, for it seems to catch in a condensed way the mental processes of differentiation and integration, the slope and the area, the one and the two dimensional which taken together generate the three-dimensional. The analogous mental process, taken away from the abstractions of mathematics or its concrete applications to the inanimate world, must use the far less precise instruments of symbols and their transformation into words. I wish here to make a differentiation that seems to grow out of the imagination about the interior world of the internal mother, the claustrum, and a certain class of phenomena which seem to deserve the names instability and rigidity. But I am aware that these same denominations apply as well to situations in which the claustrum seems to play no part. How can we differentiate and how describe the distinction?

Let us admit at the outset that any such exercise is purely in the interest of tidiness of thought and has little if anything to do with the actual events of the consulting room where two highly unique mentalities are met in love and battle. But they are also met in interest, both in themselves and in one another, and certainly there are moments in which the intensity of this interest holds together the love-making and the battling to initiate a truly passionate conjunction. It may not, does not last very long each time but its growth-promoting quality, for both, is unmistakeable. Probably most often it breaks up because the analyst errs; he misconstrues, oversteps the limits of privacy, enacts rather than communicating. But at other times the tension is too much for the patient and he retreats; the end of the session has loomed, the tension of uncertainty is unbearable, he experiences the pain as gratuitous or the pleasure as too erotic.

Generally both patient and analyst have to wait for dreams to

111

elucidate the diaspora of emotions, but even with this help from the unconscious, a certain tidiness of thought plays a role in understanding what has happened. In this respect the events of the consulting room differ in no fundamental way from the transactions of any intimate relationship. The recovery and renewal of the passionate moment determines the growth and deepening; the failure to do so marks the withering process, as areas of communication become shut off and are replaced by a tacit contract of avoidance.

It seems reasonable to suggest that between rigidity of avoidance and instability of contact there is possibly a middle zone whose stability consists essentially in the readiness to try again.

This readiness must, I would suppose, imply a mutual uncertainty of the reasons of the breakdown in intimacy and a readiness to forgive, both oneself and the other. That, in turn, requires a sophisticated attitude towards pain in which the interest in its meaning exceeds the aversion to its sensual quality, the painfulness of the pain. It is difficult to imagine this capacity to be equal in the members at any particular moment, however matched they may be overall. In that moment one member must carry the burden of optimism. Insofar as the analytic transference/countertransference has a child/parent configuration, clearly this role falls to the analyst as a matter of responsibility.

In the situation of those patients who present a claustrum way of life, I have described both their instability and their rigidity, how they rush from compartment to compartment, from grandiosity to claustrophobia, and how they rigidly construe the analytic situation as an institutional one. I have also tried to suggest a way of understanding this as a preformed transference which does not in itself generate an analytical process, indicating that this differentiation has a very beneficial effect on the analyst's stability, that is his patience, tolerance, continued interest and hopefulness. But in normal and neurotic analysands the situation is more complex. We meet not only the rigidity of splitting processes and omnipotent control, the instability of PsD, but also the eruption of projective identificatory phenomena, and attendant loss of contact.

As I say, it may be just an exercise in mental tidiness to raise the question about the structural nature of the break in contact: has a part of the personality disappeared into projective identification or has the center of gravity of identity and control of consciousness shifted to a part that is already ensconced? In the playroom the differentiation is strongly suggested in action: the child may suddenly dive into his bolt-hole under the table or couch, or he may disrupt the play he has been engaged in to construct a bolt hole, either a comfy one, a masturbation chamber, or a torture chamber. The difference between continuity and discontinuity is clearly significant, the latter indicating a failure of contact between analyst and patient, implying an analytic failure. Where the continuity of the play is preserved, the problem still remains to distinguish between concreteness of the action and dramatization for communiction. But nonetheless it would seem to be indicated that a withdrawal is being represented rather than a shift in the state of mind.

That would seem to be a significant differentiation. The discontinuity suggests a surrender, an abandonment of an effort at relationship on the patient's part and would seem to lay the problem at the analyst's feet. They both represent instability in the patient, but of two different types, one intrinsic to the economics of the transference, the other to a failure of the adequate use of the countertransference.

Discontinuities are less easily recognized with adult patients. They cannot be recognized by what appears to be a change of subject, for connecting links may have been omitted eliptically, or the patient may be engaged in a circumlocution that will eventually come back to its origin. I think it can only be detected in the countertransference, feeling the change in the atmosphere, the temperature or distance, noting a wave of loneliness or a sense of being snubbed.

Let us pretend that this distinction has been made and that it is of clinical significance, not just an exercise in tidiness. But what does it mean? We are thrown back to very fundamental problems in our working model of the mind, those dealing with the nature of consciousness and with the sense of identity. The formulation of Freud, that consciousness is an organ for the perception of psychic qualities, which Bion has embraced, may indeed shift us into Plato's cave, but it is not so simple. Once we

113

have abandoned the idea of the unity of the mind, it becomes a rather crowded cave. Perhaps there is only room for one or two parts of the personality at a time to squeeze through the portal to where the shadows on the wall become visible. I am reminded of going to great lengths to visit Altamira only to be told that application must be made in advance, with a waiting list of two years, and a requirement of some professional purpose. Or perhaps the control of the organ of consciousness is like a rugby scrum. Not only is there perhaps a problem of which part gets the ball but being able to hold onto it long enough to score. After all, do objects, either external or internal, actually "seize" our attention or do we need to focus? What is distractability? The scrum is a pretty cogent image!

In our sporting analogy we can of course move in the direction that would imply changes in organization and integration of the self. We could move, say, to tennis. Doubles, mixed doubles, singles. Or to golf, match and medal play. We soon find we need to make distinctions between playing with, playing against, or playing by oneself. If the pendulum swings too far towards integration and cooperation, under the aegis of the rules-of-the-game, it can lose the stability so gained and swing into the rigidity of isolation, obsession.

The upshot of such speculations or exercises in imagination about the mental apparatus leave us in the lurch in any attempt at an overview of the psycho-analytical process. Perhaps with refinement of our countertransference sensibilities we may be able to make this moment-to-moment distinction between continuity and discontinuity, and thus between reentry to the claustrum versus shift of consciousness and sense of identity, but I doubt that we can say with any conviction that an ensconced part of the personality has come out. It is a different matter with the delusional system of the schizophrenic. Regardless of the satisfactory nature of the remission, we can always see evidence that the system is still there, still inhabited, still influencing the state of mind, just around the corner of his conscious field.

On the whole I think we must rely on evidence which is far from precise, perhaps even largely negative evidence, namely changes in the patient's view-of-the-world. For this seems to me to be the heart of the matter. It might be said to come down to "what newspaper do you read" versus what do you consider to be evidence of the nature of the world you inhabit? We are, after all, bombarded with hearsay that declares that the world is man-made and therefore its possible destruction by man is also imminent. It is alleged to be a world of "news", composed of political, financial, gossip, sport and entertainment novelty. This appeal to membership of the basic assumption group, where the assumption is that man is the measure of all things, is either irresistibly "realistic" or manifestly absurd and repulsive, depending on one's relation to psychic reality. Either one is in a state of denial of psychic reality, ready to assume that common sense is adequate, that things are just what they seem, or one lives inside an object and naturally sees the world as a vale of tears and prison-house; or one lives in a family atmosphere dependent on the bounty and mystery of the natural world, which one may use, abuse or neglect. The only "faith" that is required is an absolute belief in one's feebleness, ignorance, impotence and mortality, to open to view the beauty-of-the-world and passionate feelings.

8 The Role of The Claustrum in the Onset of Schizophrenia *

My clinical experience over the years, of analytic work with adults and children, normal, borderline and psychotic, and a wide supervision component of my work, has resulted in the building of a model of the mind, based chiefly on the work of Freud, Abraham, Klein and Bion, in which the geographic dimension of structure is very central. The "worlds" in which human mental experience takes place are various, at least four in number, fundamentally: outside, inside and the interior of internal and external objects. To this must be added, in the case of schizophrenic phenomena, a fifth world which is essentially "nowhere", that is, having no dynamic or structural links with the other four. This I see as the world of the delusional system while the other four are dimensions of psychic reality.

Given that the human personality is never unified but variously unintegrated and riven by splitting processes, the theoretical problems encountered in the clinical approach to the schizophrenias may be seen, grossly speaking, as three in number: how does the delusional system form? how does a part or parts of the personality come to live in this "nowhere" world? and what are the factors which determine the access to consciousness of the mental state of such deluded part or parts? Here I wish to focus attention on the second of these questions, but to give it substantial texture it is necessary to indicate very briefly my approach to the other two.

The delusional system is similar to "Man's Picture of His World", in the sense of Money-Kyrle, something that is built bit by bit by "learning from experience" in Bion's sense. The delusional system is constructed bit by bit in parallel with the building of the worlds of psychic reality. But just as they are constructed through successful symbol-formation and by introjection of received symbols, the delusional system is built up from failed symbol-formation — what Bion has called the

---

*Read to the Symposium on the Psychotherapy of Schizoprenia, Stockholm, August 1991

"beta elements with traces of ego and superego", the debris of "alpha-function in reverse". I will say no more but refer the reader merely to Freud's description of the rebuilding of Schreber's world after the world-destruction phantasy and to Milton's description in *Paradise Lost* of Satan and his troop of Fallen Angels building Pandemonium on the model of Heaven but with infernal materials.

In answer to the third question, of access to consciousness of delusional material, I wish to make it clear that I am using the term "consciousness" entirely in the sense of "organ for the perception of psychic qualities" (Freud), therefore of "attention" (Bion) or perception of phenomena (Plato). Fragmentation of the self being, to a greater or lesser degree, a universal attribute of the mental apparatus, the "organ of attention" is highly prized and struggled over by the various parts of the self because of its direct access to motility (Freud), although it by no means holds a monopoly in this regard. The factors at play in this struggle for dominion over motility are a wide and fascinating area of study but, of course, outside our present efforts.

To return then to our topic — "how does a part or parts of the personality come to live in this 'nowhere' world" — we must give detailed attention to the fourth area of psychic reality: inside of internal objects, the claustrophobic world of borderline psychotic states. Knowledge of the phenomenology of the claustrophobic world comes largely from analytic work with a certain category of psychotic children, from psychotic breakdown in adolescence (often associated with drug abuse) but also, surprisingly, from the early stages of the analysis of the so-called normal and well-adjusted people who come to analysis for professional development of one sort or another (in whom the practice of senior analysts tend to abound). From these experiences it has been concluded that the entry into projective identification is an ubiquitous phenomenon in early childhood mainly instituted during conflicts over excretory processes and implemented through the phantasies of penetrating mastur-batory activities, especially anal masturbation.

While the perseverence of an infantile part living in projective identification with an internal object, usually the mother and usually at a part-object level, ordinarily merely throws up symptoms of claustrophobia/agoraphobia and manic or depressive trends in character when such an ensconced part of the personality has gained control of the organ of consciousness marked general changes occur. First of all the experience of the outside world becomes dominated by the claustrophobic atmosphere, meaning that the person, in whatever situation he finds himself, feels trapped. Job, marriage, holiday, on trains, buses or lifts, in personal or casual relations, in restaurants or theatres — in every area there is a tangible atmosphere of catastrophe immanent and "No Exit" (Sartre). Second, in response to this hovering sense of immanent catastrophe, the picture of the world becomes compartmentalized and stratified. The compartments, which have a strong phyllogenetic or at least historic flavour, resemble closely in their meaning the divisions Hell, Purgatory and Heaven: in the rectum, the genital or inside the breast or head of the primal mother. Furthermore all organization is seen as stratified, hierarchic and therefore in a sense political, whether it be family, extended family, work place; whether it be socially concrete as an institution or abstract as a class or occupation. The claustrophobic quality of mind, therefore, generates both restlessness to change geography, and/or ambition to climb some existent or non-existent social ladder, to imagined safety at the top.

It is essential to grasp the social atmosphere of the claustrophobic world in order to comprehend that it is a "place" where development of the personality cannot progress, and from which two types of exit exist, out into the world of object relations and emotional links or expulsion to the "nowhere" of the delusional system. The central item of this social atmosphere is the simplicity of the value system, survival. Survival has the meaning of evading expulsion which seems to constitute the most nameless dread of mental life. While this unitary value system of survival is most obviously persecutory in the rectal compartment (Brecht's "Fears and Miseries of the Third Reich"), it also exists in the genital compartment as compulsive greed for sexual stimulation, and in the breast compartment as a type of "Lotus Eaters" lassitude, perhaps a bit corresponding to Freud's embracing of the "nirvana principle". Correspondingly the overall attitude is intensely

119

conservative. Even in the rectum things could always be worse, but never better except by escape to one of the other two compartments or by climbing the ladder of tyrannical authority.

The second overall quality of the claustrophobic world is the sense of being fraudulent, an intruder, interloper, always in danger of being detected by the natives of this region. But in fact there are no natives, only other intruders, masquerading. The consequence, and third predominant characteristic of the milieu, is the impossibility of sincerity in relationships. At best there can be alliances, uneasy and distrustful. Communication therefore is reduced to half-truths, at best, manipulative lies or self-conscious, rehearsed presentations of the truth in a manner intended to be disbelieved. The predominant attitude towards truthfulness is that of the delinquent: anything that cannot be disproved must be taken as true. This of course engenders a background implication of incipient litigiousness.

The result of these three predominant implications for the social environment of the claustrophobic world is that emotional linkages cannot arise and are replaced, and in a manner simulated, by various states of excitement engendered by "story-telling". Should an emotional link arise, instead of its being relegated to unconscious dream processes and thought for elucidation of its meaning, an immediate story, parable, allegory or confabulation is constructed to forestall thought. As a result autonomous symbol formation is damped and dependence upon received symbols replaces dream-thought, conscious confabulation replaces unconscious thought.

It will be understood, I trust, that I am speaking of the quality of the experience of the world for that part of the personality living in the claustrum. In the borderline psychotic this may seem to be total, but, like the schizophrenic whose delusional system may seem total, this is never in fact true. There are always parts of the personality living outside the object, the clinical picture being determined by the control of consciousness, attention and motility. In the neurotic patient, and perhaps in most people generally, the existence of an infantile part still inhabiting the claustrum casts its shadow on the person's "picture of his world". Pessimism, cynicism and a belief in political solutions are its hallmarks.

As you see, I am suggesting that the problem to which I am

addressing myself — "how does a part or parts of the personality come to inhabit the 'nowhere' world of the delusional system" — can be elucidated by the assumption, strongly suggested by clinical experience and by literature, that the portal of entry lies through the state of projective identification. Perhaps any one of the three compartments within the body of the internal mother, rectum, vagina or breast/head, can serve as entrée. The problem of the formation of the delusional system and the enigma of access to consciousness I am leaving aside in this presentation, as I have said. The preliminary question of the dynamics which bring about states of projective identification have already been extensively investigated and reported by myself and others.

This brings us to the heart of the matter. I am asking you to imagine the plight of the part of the personality, necessarily an infantile part, structurally speaking, in its life in the claustrum. You will immediately have recognised a disquieting resemblance between this description of the claustrophobic world and Freud's description of the "plight of the ego serving three masters" in "The Ego and the Id". This pessimistic view of the human condition, which gives such credence to concepts such as Nirvana Principle or Death Instinct, stems from life in the claustrophobic world of projective identification, not from life in the outside world of intimate emotional relationships and the beauty and bounty of nature (with a small "n"). But it does bear this unhappy resemblance to those aspects of life in the outside world of a casual or contractual level, of business and politics, institutions and organizations.

In its unhappy state, faced with problems of survival, devoid of trusting and intimate relationships, shorn of the capacity for autonomous symbol formation and therefore of the ability for creative thought, in constant danger of being detected as an interloper and arraigned for trial and expulsion into "nowhere", the ensconced part of the personality must balance this misery with certain pleasures. These pleasures are restricted to two sorts, the fragile grandiosity which comes from the identificatory aspect of projective identification, and the delinquent pleasures of "beating the system" and evading detection as an intruder. Escape to less persecutory compartments or climbing the hierarchic ladder of the ruling organization are strenuous

121

and tenuous respites only. The literary documentation of this state is as compelling as the experience of the analytic consulting room: Shakespeare, Milton, Coleridge, Strindberg, Kafka, Pinter, Dostoievsky, to name a few.

Into this unhappy state the memory of two other prior states enters as a continual torment of the Paradise Lost type: life in the womb and the life of intimate emotional relationships (at root, the breast-feeding one), with its delight of thought and growth through learning from experience of emotional meaning. The claustrophobic world is, indeed, the Vale of Tears and not Keats's "Vale of Soul-making".

Eventually, perhaps inevitably, the dreaded event of detection of the intruder ensues, the trial and the expulsion into the "nowhere" of the delusional system. In order to make this process clinically vivid, I will present an outline of the experience by a woman therapist, Mrs. Catharine Mack Smith, trained at the Tavistock Clinic, in which I had the happy experience as supervisor, with a boy Daniel, from age eight to thirteen, with an unexpected follow-up of two sessions eight years later, age twenty-one.

I will try to describe briefly a therapy which lasted four years, varying from four times per week to twice and sometimes only once, depending on the oscillating enthusiasm of mother and special school. At the start Daniel presented as a tall and well-built boy, expressionless in face, rigid in movements, toneless of voice and with large, frighteningly blank black eyes. Outwardly polite and docile, his mode of cooperation was to sit and draw simple pictures of people and animals while he talked of the relationships, mainly factual but unintelligible because of continual transpositions of the men-on-foxes-hunt-mice variety. His state of mind was made most clear during the first year by a drawing of a fox in his hole and a rabbit at the opening who was telling him what was happening outside, but tricking him by telling it all wrong. Exploration of his state of projective identification elicited evidence that this was the nature of his slavish dependence on his older brother and had existed from early on, the method of mocking Daniel was by feeding him false information.

The relationship to the therapist began to develop from this point and seemed to reach a climax of confidentiality over a drawing of a person fishing through a hole in the ice and catching a fish, but by mistake, as it were, hooking it by the tail. Daniel's educability at school increased and the behaviour in therapy became very complex and variable. His brother now figured as his bête noire while a child at school became, correspondingly, Daniel's victim of ceaseless teasing — at least so his talk indicated, as he swung between rage at his brother and sadistic giggling about the schoolmate (an epileptic child, in fact). This split between the tormented part inside the object and the tormenter outside was also represented by behaviour on the couch and under the couch. But there was also a middle position, on the floor with legs under the couch, occupied with making lists of information drawn from an atlas, an encyclo- paedia or from memory. An obsessional interest in history and geography emerged. Again the information fluctuated from precise to grossly distorted at various times.

As these structural situations were explored and the transference implication of curiosity about the therapist's history and internal geography was suggested, masturbatory activities, oral, anal and genital emerged, accompanied more and more by sadistic preoccupations with war, murder, slaughter of animals, and rape. Passionate ambivalence appeared in connection with holiday breaks and the strain on the therapist mounted towards the breaking point. But the newspaper report of the murder of a woman named Joy seemed to break Daniel's capacity for emotional contact.

For the following year and one half, the obsessional position took over almost completely, with endless lists, covert mastur- bation, refusal of response to interpretation, leaving sessions early, claiming he had nothing interesting to say, and finally demanding the end of the therapy. The mother seemed relieved, the school rather neutral and the therapist exhausted and heartbroken.

Eight years later Daniel unexpectedly reappeared asking for a session, apparently at the suggestion of a psychiatrist who had seen him in the local mental hospital and thought that a resumption of therapy was a possibility. But Daniel had not come for treatment but to inform and instruct his former therapist so that she might be able to help other children where she had failed with him. He presented now as a strongly-built

123

six foot tall young man, looking quite mad and frighteningly so, the big blank eyes now aggressively staring and challenging. The story he told in the two sessions he requested was as follows: at a certain point in the therapy he had to come under the influence of "evil beings". They had ordered him to keep a diary which was not to be shown or mentioned to anyone, especially the therapist, under pain of being tried and hanged. This diary began to occupy more and more of his time and eventually, as it invaded his hours at school, a teacher had removed it from him summarily. Accordingly he was tried and hanged, which meant also that he must commit suicide the next day. But in despair he had prayed to "The Great God of the Inner World" who had agreed to spare him. Ever since he had loved the Great God and been loved by him.

That was all told in the first session. The second was devoted to an account of his current activities and difficulties. He lived at home with his mother, step-father having died and brother moved away. Periodically he went into mental hospital when his mother needed a rest from him. His main activities were writing and studying, as he is writing both a novel and a study of the social life of wolves. His main trouble consists of outbreaks of shouting abuse, at any time and any place. This abusive language consists of all the things he should have shouted at the time, age thirteen, when a girl at school humiliated him. He did not itemize the abuse he now hurled at her.

In addition to these activities and items of behaviour, he has a mission in life (perhaps under orders from the Great God) to encourage women to learn karate so that they may be able to defend themselves from thieves, attackers and rapists. (It had been a feature of his material during the analysis when the masturbation was at its height that girls were at least as strong as boys, and women probably stronger than men.)

The events of the therapy over these four years from the time Daniel was almost nine until age thirteen were excruciatingly slow and boringly repetitive due to the diffuse obsessionality of his post-autistic state. In the first year, in which he did little else but make simple drawings accompanied by monotone descriptions in which everything was misnamed, he related very little to the therapist and reacted hardly at all to the structure and variations of the analytic situation. The elucidation of his claustrophobic state through the drawings of innumerable animals in holes in the ground, and of his persecution by a big brother figure outside teasing him with misinformation, seemed to release a part of his personality to emerge from the claustrum and enter into an infantile transference relationship to the therapist. But at times the part which had emerged also became the cruel big brother to the part still inside, the split being represented by lying drawing with his legs under the couch, and acted out by tormenting the epileptic boy at school.

As Daniel's educability increased it was overshadowed by his obsessionality and preoccupation with time (history) and geography (space) as dimensions of his transference relationships to the maternal object. Puberty overtook him very rapidly, the transference became fraught with the pregenital and genital sexuality, predominantly anal sadistic in content with perverse destructiveness towards the mother's internal babies. In retrospect, according to his later communication, various external and internal events occurred which shut down the therapy and brought into prominence the delusional system: the girl who humiliated him (how?), the emergence of the "evil beings" who commanded him to keep a secret diary which gradually took up more and more of his time, the removal of the diary by the teacher which resulted in his trial, hanging and command to commit suicide, his prayer to the "God of the Inner World" who pardoned him and whom he has since "loved'. His grandiose delusional mission, presumably in the service of this God, is to encourage all women to learn karate to defend against the violence of male perversity, represented in his shouting attacks of abusive language.

Thus there has come into existence what we estimate to be his present personality structure: the schizophrenic part of his personality, in love with the "God of the Inner World" has a grandiose delusional mission; a perverse big-brother part breaks forth in abusive shouting attacks on the girl who humiliated him, and by implication, all females; a more evolved but deeply obsessional part which is engaged in writing a novel and a tract on the family life of wolves. One presumes that his love for the "Great God" is feminine, like Schreber's, and that his mission is of a feminist anti-masculine nature. Eight years later we have lost sight of the "little brother" part, still inside

125

and being tormented, which had been represented by the epileptic boy.

In closing this chapter I cannot resist taking up a bit more space to tell you and commend to your attention a most remarkable play by the young Harold Pinter. Written in the early sixties when, along with *The Caretaker*, he was exploring the world of paranoia and insanity, *The Birthday Party* is a dream-play, created with such economy and precision of language that it lends itself to analysis line-by-line in a breathtaking way.

In brief, it is the story of a young man, Stanley, who, after giving his only piano recital in a local hall, hugely unnoticed and unsuccessful, has taken refuge in a seaside boarding house run by Meg and her husband. Here he lives in a bedroom and the kitchen, where he is constantly hovered over by the solicitous, placental Meg whose conversation is limited to anxious questions such as, "Are the cornflakes good this morning?" Into this retreat, where Stanley is the only lodger, and his only companionship is with his sisterly "girlfriend's" occasional visits, there enter two travelling salesmen, just for the night, Goldberg and McCann (who seem to represent the Church and Synagogue in their most political aspects). It is Stanley's birthday and it is celebrated by a wild party during the course of which he is browbeaten, his glasses smashed, the drum Meg has given him is destroyed and his girlfriend is seduced by Goldberg (as she reports the next morning, "He taught me things a girl shouldn't know until she's been married three times.") By this time Stanley has been reduced to sightless mutism and is taken away to be cured, "To Monty" (Monte Carlo or Field Marshal Montgomery?). Curtain!

Just to remind you by way of recapitulation: in this chapter I have addressed myself to the middle of three problems in the elucidation of schizophrenia: how does the delusional system come into existence, how do parts of the personality become alienated into this "nowhere", and what determines the ability of such an alienated part to take control of the organ of consciousness, and thus of a large area of behaviour? The answer I have suggested and illustrated is perhaps to be found in the detailed illumination of the world of projective identi-fication inside the body/mind of the internal mother, the "claustrum".

9   Concerning the Ubiquity of Projective Identification

When Melanie Klein first described the omnipotent phantasy of projective identification it appeared as an exotic, a rare psychotic phantasy involving external objects and deep alienation of the sense of identity. Forty-five years of research, clinical experience with children and adults and a wide experience of baby observation have not only demonstrated its elementary function with internal objects but have made clear the wide range of phenomena, both useful for relationships and communication or wildly pathological, that come within this broad description of narcissistic identification processes.

Infant observation in particular strongly suggests its essential nature in the preverbal period as the mediator between the baby's confusional states and the mother's capacity for reverie and unconscious dream-thought. A view of the developmental process that emphasizes structure of self and objects in the light of splitting processes must necessarily take into consideration the unevenness of development: that those parts of the self which make contact with external figures are most likely to establish enduring relations with internal objects and benefit from the facilitation, through thought, of learning from experience, that is from emotional experiences. But other parts of the personality do not develop this capacity for intimacy, must learn by other routes and are forced thereby relentlessly towards adaptation rather than development. Of these other parts, relatively estranged or absolutely estranged from the heart of the internal family structure, one or another is perhaps left behind at each developmental step ("step" is more appropriate than "point" because the developmental process, as represented in psychoanalysis, certainly makes leaps of comprehension and acceptance — Wittgenstein's "now I can go on"). Clinical differentiation suggests that parts may be left behind in the womb, producing states of withdrawal quite different in phenomena from those of projective identification. Clearly some are left behind in the claustrum in which they have taken refuge or into which they have penetrated. In the chapter on "Emergence from the Claustrum" the question of entrapment has been investigated: is the portal of entry really closed against exit?

The task of comprehensive description of the role of projective identification in personality functioning cannot escape the complexity of the problem. First of all there is the spectrum of maturity of parts involved, ranging from neonate to adolescent. Second there is the quality of the parts, perhaps best described in terms of plus and minus L, H and K, or in terms of warmth and coldness, or in terms of need of contact versus isolation. And finally there is the variation contingent on the compartment of the claustrum and on mobility from one compartment to another. All three of these variables are modified in their clinical visibility by a fourth factor: control of the organ of consciousness, attention.

Probably no individual personality is ever simple, for it would appear that splitting processes are possibly the very first move in the warding off of mental pain. This possibility has been explored in the *The Apprehension of Beauty* where it was suggested that the initial emotional experience of the newborn is an unbearably powerful passionate response to the beauty of the world, modified only by the reciprocity of the nursing mother. If, as the echographic studies of the foetus strongly suggest, personality development begins in utero and birth is an emotional experience, no regressive move would be more understandable than to go back, in phantasy, to one's earlier home inside. But even in early infancy the forms of the outside world would have already set their stamp on the phantasised qualities of this interior world. Truly the whole complex structure of the internal mother's interior would take time and experience to develop, as we discovered in following the evolution of Doreen Weddell's "Barry" (*Explorations in Autism*), but the perception of the forms of the external world mould unconscious phantasy in an irresistible fashion. (Is there such a thing as an "imaginary animal" or only one compounded of fragments of reality, a bizarre object? Consider the paradoxical juxtapositions in Surrealist art.)

Given, therefore, these four variables — maturity of the ensconced part(s), their quality, their compartment(s) and their possession of the organ of attention (and therefore of control of behaviour) — the task of a comprehensive description that would be of use in the consulting room is a daunting one. Maturity and qualities belongs to the general model of the mind and the question of compartments has to some extent been covered already. In this chapter the implications of control of consciousness and of behaviour and the influence on sense of identity is our central task. Within this purview must be included the general problem of stability and the particular problem of view-of-the-world.

The general problem of stability is best illustrated in the fleeting mental states of the very young child and of the adolescent. The extent of splitting processes is clearly visible in these age groups and is seen to be utterly dependent on both external circumstances and physiological states. Hunger, thirst, chilling or overheating, physical pain or discomfort, and the interpersonal climate produce wide shifts in mental state. Mood, variations in irritability, emotional responsiveness and activity of phantasy and thought can be seen to vary in clusters whose immediacy appear to be quite separate from the history of the individual and his relationships. The lack of continuity, and therefore of responsibility of each state for the consequences of the other, marks these as divorced from one another by splitting processes. In the adolescent, confrontation with such responsibility produces a "brother's keeper" sense of injustice that quite baffles parents and teachers. "I forgot" is given as absolute alibi and "I don't remember" as conclusive proof that the wrong criminal has been arrested. The impression that the pleasure principle has ousted paranoid-schizoid and depressive values is unmistakeable and would seem to be a major factor in this instability, placing the supervising adult world effectively in a more stand-by position, which, by and large, it tends to accept with more or less patience.

But in latency children and grown-ups a greater stability is evident and the appearance of instability falls more within the constant fluctuations of paranoid-schizoid and depressive positions, with a retained sense of continuity and responsibility, however grudging. Where the greater instability reflects splitting processes, the picture-of-the-world can be seen to change markedly from state to state. Consequently the appearance of claustrophobic configurations is unmistakeable. The nocturnal anxieties of the small child and the attitude towards home in the adolescent are their outstanding manifestations. It seems likely, from clinical evidence, that the quality of sleep and related dreaming are of particular importance in determining the waking state of a claustrophobic sort. The masturbation chamber mode of going to sleep seems to promote sleeping-inside-the-object and produces hardship in awakening and a state of confusion for some period, "until I shave" or "have had my coffee". The characteristic dreaming of the claustrophobic state will be described in a separate chapter.

Unfortunately there are two quite separate types of stability that must concern us here: the stability of the normal, well-adjusted person capable of making and deepening his intimate relationships and pursuing his emotional interests; and the stability of the borderline psychotic. This latter also deserves a chapter of its own, because the transference situation presented in analysis and the technical requirements are of central interest to this book. But it is necessary to pay some attention to the influence upon the "normal" person, by which we can include most non-psychotic people, of the existence of an infantile part dwelling within an internal object.

It has been displayed in the chapter on the compartments that the formal qualities of the different areas of the claustrum derive from the social organization of the outside world. What these compartments lack in particular is the atmosphere of family life, and therefore a clear differentiation between adults and children with regard to capabilities, prerogatives, responsibilities and experience. These dimensions are completely replaced by hierarchy. In the outside world, outside family life, where hierarchy exists (which is nearly universal), a certain degree of modification of privilege by knowledge, experience, skill can be seen to operate where the tasks are real, quantifiable, concrete. As soon as the task is organizational, abstract, or ethical, judgment has to fight a losing battle against status; tyranny and submission win the field. The work-group, which fortunately continues to exist even under the most savage circumstances, is forced underground, into informality and intuitive organization.

Because the compartments of the claustrum have more or less clearly defined boundaries and markedly different atmospheres and preoccupations, one of the most distinct influences cast over a person's view-of-the-world by a part living in projective identification is the tendency to see the outside world as similarly sharply demarcated. This bounding can be divided into the world of criminality, perversion, poverty and disease; the world of sexuality and procreation (not including family life but as a statistic); and the world of wealth, leisure, security and sensual, non-sexual, pleasure. We are dealing here with attitudes, often conscious, more often unconscious and variously denied. The sectioning of our newspapers and the distinctions between "news" — papers and tabloids tell the story convincingly. All our prejudices belong to this category — of colour, religion, ethnic groups, geographic areas, professions, political attitudes; our choice of where to live, to which schools to send our children, our holiday choices, entertainments, reading, choice of clothing, motor car, spouse.

But to say that our prejudices belong to this category is merely to say that prejudices are attitudes which are not based on experience and thought but correspond to infantile values which have been embraced second-hand, taken over from those we consider above us in the hierarchic system, prejudgments both for and against other people, animals, vegetables, gods and phenomena. Interpreting all prejudice in terms of states of projective identification does not mean that the content of the prejudice is determined by the qualities of the interior world, but rather that the degree of conviction — the urgency and the sharpness of distinctions — is influenced thereby. Another way of putting it would be to say the seriousness with which we entertain our unconsidered judgments and the degree to which they are allowed to influence our actions in the world derive from parts living in projective identification.

Perhaps to clarify this point we could examine the lexical aspects of prejudice, of unexamined attitudes, often unnoticed values. One could draw up a list of the adverbs of unobservant un-thought: clearly, obviously, self-evident, of course, naturally, we think, how else, what could you expect, as I always say, where there's smoke, not like us, etc. etc. etc. "Everyone" thinks, knows, believes, is certain. Observation and thought cannot come to such termini, cannot close its books to further evidence, must always act hesitantly, ready to retract, to regret.

131

The reasons for this are strongly suggested by the findings of psycho-analysis: that only a small portion of what we observe is noticed consciously, and only a tiny portion of the operations of unconscious mental processes can be made visible to our organ of attention. Like it or not, and with our great craving for self control it is difficult to like, we must operate on trust in these internal workings, vigilant for the parapraxes of thought and attitude as well as action.

In our intimate relationships we do indeed exercise this vigilance and note the parapraxes which hurt our loved ones, impede our passionate interest and bring us to apparently paradoxical impasse. But in our adaptational life in the world of casual and contractual relationships and interests, we are not thus moved to observation and thought. We are obliged to operate within one hierarchy and another, we are forced to accept membership in various groups, we are subject to vast pressure to conform to the order of tyranny and submission, alarmed only when that which is demanded is clearly degrading to the personae of our intimate lives. We are tempted to yield to degradation while keeping such actions secret from those we love, unless our awareness of internal figures precludes such devices. Every love object being a hostage to fate, when "everything threatens the head that I love"; the problem of Caesar and Christ, Luther's Two-Kingdoms, is always with us.

So what can it mean to say that we must resist taking our received, unthought-out attitudes too seriously? First of all we must resist having a view-of-the-world, the temptation to that great generalization which goes so infinitely beyond our actual experiences of the limited events that we can actually observe and allow our minds to digest in thought. We become aware of this in foreign travel, where, not really speaking the language, only seeing the culture on show to its tourist trade, even if we work abroad, it is brought home to us. Travel is broadening in that it shows us how little we know of the world, and of our own culture, when noting differences makes us pay attention to what has passed unnoticed and been taken for granted at home.

Second, it should be possible to avoid the tendency to compartmentalize our own life processes in the way that seems to make us into different people in different circumstances, taking the uniform seriously of work, of play, of the sexual community. The propaganda is terrific — to rush away from home in order to have a holiday; to display our work status by home, car, clothing and demeanour; to keep fit in order to display our sexual prowess and satisfaction. The compartmentalized attitude would be clearly claustrophobic were we not to dispel this aspect of the problem by rushing from compartment to compartment. And beyond this frantic aspect of the claustrum, colouring our lives from that unconscious infantile level, is the hypochondriac consequence of the identificatory aspect of projective identification upon which anxiety the constant din of health propaganda is continually directed by the media and the drug companies.

Stripped of the illusory value of rushing from one compartment to another, and stripped of the attention we are badgered into paying to status, the level of economic prosperity yields very little of essential value, nor do alterations of the economic factors in our lives carry much anxiety. It is all too evident that these fluctuations are national, sometimes world-wide, and utterly impersonal, little understood and beyond significant control. Clearly the best political system is the one with least power to impose itself on the individual and intrude its way into the private, intimate lives of its citizens. The Socratic ideal of the just man, who knows what is his business and minds it, limits us to activity in the small area of personal observation and experience. Beyond that it is all hearsay. The job that we do in the world is, truly, part of our business, but we can avoid the cobbler's view that the happiness of the world depends on everyone having good shoes. If we are lucky enough to have jobs that capture our passionate interest, we are just lucky, for any thoughtful examination of how we attained such positions soon reveals the blindness with which we stumbled into them in the naiveté and inexperience of youth.

But the influence exerted on our attitudes and interests by an infant part left in projective identification runs absolutely counter to minding one's own business. The compart-mentalized view-of-the-world sets up an obsessive interest in the "others", particularly those supposed to live in different compartments than oneself: the rich, the aristocratic, the powerful, the beautiful, the famous, the dying, the criminal, the pervert. The salacious ill-will of such typically interior

133

preoccupations are, of course, richly catered for. Where the mobility from compartment to compartment of an ensconced part is limited, the longing is accompanied by an idealization of these "others" — the "freedom" of those in the gutter, the wantonness of those in the erotic community, the indolent parasitism of the aristocrat/intelligentsia.

Just as certain aspects of upbringing seem to favour a borderline personality of the interior type — wealth, beauty, aristocracy in particular — so there are circumstances of everyday life which are revealed by dreams as exerting a tendency for the state of mind to shift into the projective mode, affecting mood, attitudes and impulse life at the moment: groups of which one is not a willing member, failures of public services, situations where one finds oneself an intruder, an unintentional voyeur or tempted to appropriate items of monetary value. Any situation in which one is or feels "classified" by an invisible bureaucracy, whether engendering a sense of elitism or of degradation, jogs one's stability. Any event which seems to threaten one's illusion of security nudges one into the claustrum. Because the capacity for observation and thought is immediately curtailed by such a shift in sense of identity, the impulse to act is very exigent. Where immediate action is precluded by circumstance, the alternative is to master the emotion by making a story of the situation with a view to future retailing. This not only further hampers thought but, by packaging the event in contrived meaning, actually prevents the experience being digested into thought in the unconscious. By sealing the observed/imagined events into linguistic form, it substitutes recall for the creative processes of memory.

In summary, psycho-analytical experience with children and adults strongly suggests that the existence of one or another infantile part either living in projective identification or easily provoked to enter the claustrum of internal objects is fairly ubiquitous. Every analysis begins with copious material referable to the sewer, the erotic encounter or parasitic bliss, as soon as the preformed transference has been dispelled so that some degree of intimacy can be allowed.

10   Symptomatology versus Characterology — Psycho-analytical Process

The view of the analytical process that I have utilized and written about these many years is one that stresses the resolution of confusional states as the necessary prelude to the threshold of the depressive position. Of the many types of confusion that can be given a name for descriptive purposes, all can be classified, for theoretical purposes, under the headings of geographic and zonal confusions. This has not only the advantage of orderliness, since the descriptive variations are fairly limitless, but also has a certain utility in the consulting room. For instance, to see good/bad confusions as the result of inadequate splitting-and-idealization has an imaginative appeal, but does not easily lend itself to clinical exemplification; on the other hand to define it as a zonal confusion, for instance faeces confused with penis, or as a consequence of projective identification, a bad part of the self having intruded into the paternal penis, finds immediate realization in dreams or children's play.

With the advent of the threshold of the depressive position, the truly genital oedipus complex makes its appearance on centre stage for the first time, having been so admixed with pregenital elements previously that the struggle towards acceptance of the combined object and the sacrosanct privacy of the nuptial chamber in psychic reality could not yet take shape. The reasons for this did not reside only in the various confusional states of the self but also in the state of the internal objects due to splitting of good from bad qualities, as for instance the top from the bottom of the maternal object, and by their contamination by projective identifications by split-off parts of the self. Both the improved integration of the internal parents and their clarification, or rehabilitation, by withdrawal of the intrusions are products of the analytic working through, that is, of the transference/countertransference process.

Under this model the phenomena of the consulting room with borderline patients present the prolonged period of preformed institutional transference that has been described, while the

manic-depressive patient presents an oscillation of compart-
mental states alternating with the obsessional interval described
by Abraham in which a true familial transference ensues. In
such patients the struggle with what was formerly called massive
projective identification, but which I am now more inclined to
see as a problem of control over attention and the organ of
consciousness, is of long duration and problematic in its outcome. With normal and neurotic patients the initial work with
geographic confusion is of relatively short duration and
establishes the differentiation of analysand and analyst
regarding functions, prerogatives and expectations. It is most
clearly seen with children but comparable acting in the
transference is not difficult to distinguish with adult patients as
well. It is in the run-up to the threshold of the depressive
position that the main body of the analytic work takes place. It
is a growth process which is by no means brought to a halt by the
advent of the threshold, nor by the termination of the analysis,
but is in fact life-long. It bears some separate treatment here, for
it is a source of very considerable confusion, in the minds of
both patients and analysts, regarding the nature and aims of the
analytical process.

Once the analytical situation has been established, first by the
gathering of sufficient infantile familial transference to make for
continuity, during which period also the necessary frequency of
sessions can be ascertained, and the differentiation of the
identity, prerogatives and expectations of analysand and
analyst have been sufficiently established that the acting in the
transference has given way, at least partially, to cooperation
and communication, the panorama of the patient's extended
metapsychology begins to be laid out for view. Due to splitting
processes certain areas of infantile transference and modes of
relationship may remain enacted outside the sessions and only
revealed anecdotally or in dreams, but nonetheless the
analysand's character and the character of the analyst begin to
mingle and clash. The rhythm of the separations brings a
corresponding rhythm of acting in and out, alternating with
communication, intimacy, confidentiality, criticism. Freud's
dictum that the neurosis is converted to a transference neurosis
seems only partially true because those aspects of character that
derive from infantile configurations and conflicts continue to be

manifest in all areas of the analysand's life, not only in the analysis.

The picture that gradually emerges with adult patients presents a deceptive homogeneity from which emanates a particular atmosphere with its own individual flavour — an idiosyncratic colouring, speaking analogically. It defies description, cannot be dissected into its components, for its cultural and individual qualities, its adult and infantile attributes are all blended together. Like the first act of *Uncle Vanya*, it is difficult to imagine anything happening in this turgid state. But gradually the dramatis personae of the analysand's history, his current life situation, expectations of the future, and the figures of his internal world as compared to the external, begin to declare themselves. The areas of confusion and conflict begin to make sparks in the consulting room and the dreams to particularize these sparks of emotionality. The pains and the pleasures of life begin to appear as experiences in the analysis rather than mere accounts or dramatizations of the joys and fears.

Once this has commenced, two things become apparent: that the psychological symptomatology is actually part of the character, writ large and particularized, while the psychosomatic states stand out as utterly unassimilated to mental life. One can hardly define the stresses or emotional experiences which seem to exacerbate or ameliorate them. As the analyst begins to be able to see that the psychological symptoms are particular manifestations of the general character, he also begins to discern how the atmosphere, flavour, colouring is compounded. For the alternation of acting in and out with periods of (generally mid-week) cooperation and communication, begin to dissect the adult from the infantile components.

During this period the analyst can construe, largely from negative evidence, that the patient's life processes outside the analysis have begun to improve, so that episodes of acting out, which lacerate the relative calm of his life, become apparent to the analysand as well as the analyst. The part played by other persons' qualities may blur the picture temporarily, but where genuine acting out is involved not only can the particular incident be related to the evolution of the transference, but the provocation can usually be seen to rest with the patient. Clearly the analyst cannot define any anecdote of disturbance as acting out unless he can see its relevance to the current transference/countertransference situation. Gradually he becomes able to recognize the incipience of acting out and can help the patient to avoid such events, mainly by becoming familiar with the rattle of irritability and impedence of sincerity in the consulting room.

In this section, truly the body of the analytical process, as the zonal confusions make themselves known and their sorting out by the patient's thought and thinking — illuminated at times by the analyst's interpretation of the transference evidence — forges ahead, the delineation of the parts of the self is possible. This is not only the result of the accumulation of the evidence, but also because the blending, the internal group and gang formation, begins to break up. The individuality of the different parts asserts itself and becomes known. In a general way they can be particularized here, but in each analysis they derive their separate identities from their most colourful and in a sense poetic representation in dreams and acting. Depending on the extensiveness of the fragmentation of the personality due to splitting processes, these parts are recognizable in terms of sex, erogenous zone primacy, age level, degree of adherence to the good objects as against narcissistic alienation, by the geography of their life space (with respect to the particular model of the mind in use).

The analyst is now in a position to appreciate the uniqueness of the individual patient and the futility of classification. Of course it is what makes every analysis different and the commencement of each so daunting. We, patient and analyst, have now an opportunity to recognize the elements that make for stability, instability, rigidity, for strength, weakness or brutality, for carelessness or precision in observation and thought, for isolation, sociability or charisma. Richness or poverty of the personality, however, would seem to stem from the qualities of the internal objects, as does the prevailing value system. It should be remembered that while the delineation of paranoid-schizoid and depressive system has an overall implication of differential in values, egocentricity versus object love and concern, within the depressive position there is perhaps a limitless range for the ethical evolution. The changing ethical values of God in the Old and New Testaments bear witness to this evolutionary possibility.

It is at this time in the analysis, when the splitting of the self becomes delineated and the processes of integration are set in motion by the evolution of the transference/countertrans-ference, that the analyst can begin to see how infantile parts which are either ensconced within internal objects or have facile access to them under stress, particularly of separation, cast their influence on the character of the analysand. Here the aspect of our model of the mind which depicts compartments within the interior of the internal maternal object helps greatly to make an organized picture of a highly complicated situation. Unlike the borderline patient whose view-of-the-world emerges with a shocking clarity in its Proustian, Oblomovian, erotomanic or behind-enemy-lines qualities, in the normal and neurotic no such starkly claustrophobic picture emerges. Instead we find trends, and an occasional outburst of the claustrophobic world at moments of acting out. They now emerge as aspects of the infantile transference — the elitism, the parasitism and indolence, erotomanic transference — as well as feelings of persecution and entrapment by the analytic method, the community and the person of the analyst. But by this time such trends and outbursts are contained by the growing strength of both the positive transference and the enriched participation in the analytic work by the adult part of the personality.

The identificatory aspects of the intrusive identification, the sense of elitism, richness, powerful sexual attractiveness and superior intellect, variously show themselves as character trends. But they also reveal, in their identificatory basis, aspects of the internal objects which have been altered, and, in a sense, damaged by the intrusion. This is very clearly reflected in the transference and is eventually revealed with some frankness as the adult cooperation and sincerity improves. The analyst begins to be allowed to know many things that the patient has observed, overheard, read about and suspected bearing on the analyst's character and way of life which have been kept secret earlier. The technical problems raised by these revelations, which are also a form of interrogation, call for a firm contact with the countertransference. For after all most of the patient's suspicions or misgivings have more than a grain of truth in them. It is of course helpful to make a clear distinction between what is public knowledge and what is private. But most important, the analyst is obliged by this investigation by the patient to understand that it is part of the process of differentiating external from internal figures, and thus in the service of distinguishing the analyst as a person from the figures of the transference with which he is invested.

In many ways this interrogation, based on an increase in the patient's honesty, is also a manifestation of greater, not lesser, trust and seems often a prelude to the revelation of important secret areas in the patient's life and habits, particularly those related to the rectal compartment of intrusive identification, namely the perverse and addictive trends. They are first cautiously revealed in the dreams. While not acknowledged as related to external reality, neither is this denied. I think it can be said with some confidence that, where this situation exists, that there are secret perversions and addictions, not merely infantile polymorphous tendencies nor habitual use of stimulants or soft drugs, but areas dedicated to sado-masochism in one form or another, that the threshold of the depressive position cannot be achieved by the analysand.

The reasons for this are two-fold: one reason relates to the unconscious meaning of the perverse/addictive area; the other relates to the essential distance from and impedence of dependence on good objects that this secrecy entails. But in a certain sense both of these factors are secondary to the damaged quality of the objects consequent to the intrusive identification. This is a factor which shows itself also in the altered view-of-the-world of which I have spoken at some length. But if one examines the implications of this altered view, it can be recognized to be a reflection of the nature of the compartment(s) as a world. What does it imply for the evaluation of the qualities of these objects, essentially internal but reflected also in the transference that their interior world should be of such character, whether it be head/breast, genital or rectum? In its concrete form, as seen in the claustrophobic aspects of the phenomena generated by intrusive identification, there is displayed before us an interior world which also implies a certain level of mentality, character, values: hierarchy, elitism, privilege, exploitation, moral condemnation, expectations of obedience, punitiveness as a pedagogical method, conservatism, puritanism, hypocrisy, philistinism. In a word, minus LHK, the world of anti-emotion and anti-thought.

These are the elements of which the analyst is suspected in the crypto-pervert. But they are also suspected in the normal and neurotic with secret sado-masochistic trends. While in the latter such implications of the unrevealed dossier of observations, information and gossip may only be held to be blemishes on the surface of a bright transference object, these blemishes obstruct the aesthetic experience, the coming together in all the heat of love and hate, held in dynamic relation by the strength of the desire to know and understand.

Undoubtedly the tendencies, through masturbatory processes, to enter into intrusive identification with internal objects, have their origin in the earliest weeks and months of post-natal life. That they have a connection, a reference to memories of life in the womb can be assumed, but the great difference has been traced. It has also been suggested that states of mind influenced by intrusive indentification may be very different from those related to a split-off part of the self which has not been born, left behind, a victim of premature splitting processes, like the little crippled boy who was left behind when the Pied Piper led all the children into the mountain.

> 'Did I say, all? No, one was lame,
>   And could not dance the whole of the way;
> And in after years, if you would blame
>   His sadness, he was used to say, —
> 'It's dull in our town since my playmates left!
> 'I can't forget that I'm bereft
> 'Of all the pleasant sights they see,
> 'Which the Piper also promised me.
> 'For he led us, he said, to a joyous land,
> 'Joining the town and just at hand,
> 'Where waters gushed and fruit trees grew
> 'And flowers put forth a fairer hue,
> 'And everything was strange and new; . . .'

In considering the role of intrusive identification in the phenomena of adolescence, it seems necessary to consider the adolescent community as a whole, then those who are "over the top" (and in fact into the bottom) and also those who are left behind. Browning's description of what the Piper promised, in its great resemblance to Milton's depiction of the Garden of Eden, is a vibrant picture of the vision pursued by the adolescent community. In its developmental function, this socialization of internal processes can be viewed as experimental, essentially as experiments in departing from the protection, services and regulations, behavioural and ethical, of family life. For it to be safe, ties must not be severed, there must remain a home-base, a room of one's own in the family, even if unoccupied because of having found a "room of one's own" elsewhere.

But it is just this word "safe" that is anathema to the adolescent, for his new size, bodily development and sexual potency make him feel invulnerable. The dangers of which he has heard his parents preach in the past are seen in the light of devices for control, analogous to hell-fire preaching. The communal quality of the new experiences gives an aura of universality, the joyousness an atmosphere of purity, and the readiness for new relationships a flavour of innocence. Restraints are enslavements, the future is simply the present extrapolated. The plethora of fantasy disguises the poverty of imagination.

Within this communal atmosphere the fluidity of projective identifications is encouraged to allay the confusional states of multiple splitting processes. In the clique, the gang, the group roles shift with the changing light so that like-mindedness seems to replace any awareness of compliance with the leader of the moment. Instability and promiscuity take on the guise of friendliness, shattered only when rivalries break through in unmistakeable fashion. The reality of slavish conformity is hidden by the infinite tolerance of trivial idiosyncrasy.

This apparent safety of the group is necessary for the developmental experiments which must be made, fundamentally a review and reworking of all the evolutionary conflicts of childhood. Since they have moved "out" and "into the world" a view-of-the-world differing from that implicit in parental attitudes towards the ambience outside the family must be constructed. The first casualty of this break-out is the ethical distinction of good and bad, assumed to be behavioural in parental terms. It becomes fluid, relative. Yet it remains behavioural, therefore moral rather than ethical, for the latter requires both penetration and a capacity for abstraction and symbol formation. These qualities are temporarily lost in the heat of the freedom from tradition. In a strange way language becomes very concrete and at the same time fluid, so that argumentation tends to lose its anchorage in observation and experience and becomes a duel of verbal facility, of aggressive assertion, and moral blackmail where the implication of cowardice is intimidating above all. "Put up or shut up!" and "Put your money where your mouth is!" closes the debate. Hearsay, facts, statistics are delivered like hammer-blows.

This world-consciousness, so verbal and facile, produces a politicizing of thought and polarization of the sense of identity. Its freedom to wander off into mysticism, utopianism and nihilism is unchecked by emotional imagination but remains within the limitless battlefield of opinion. Contempt for the Establishment does not extend to discernment of the spuriousness of political methodology but remains at a simple class-warfare level, even though the classes may be different from the historic or traditional. The basic classes are the old and the young, locked in remorseless battle, oblivious of time; that today's old are yesterday's young and, heaven forbid, vice versa.

This communal state of obscured confusion seems absolutely necessary for the working over of the developmental confusions which bar the way to individuality and intimate relationships. And for most participants they succeed, at least temporarily, even though the later stresses of earning a living, constructing a family and raising children may knock them back into conformity, conservatism, timidity, and the waning of imagination in favour of denial of psychic reality. The necessity of routine for adaptation so easily turns into ritual and saps the emotionality of grown-up life. Thinking is so tiring!

Of those children who are left behind by this communalizing process, some of course are simply clinging to a rather rigid and enthusiastically approved latency period. We are not concerned with them, for they seem to go underground to the adolescent community, hoping to surface in the future when they have established themselves in the community to take up the postponed problems of sexuality. But others are left behind in the sense that their inability to socialize their rebellion leaves them in the lurch, cut off by secrecy from both family life and behavioural participation. Generally speaking they become holed-up, in a masturbation chamber either at home or in digs, largely unable to study, only able to hold down jobs far below their mental ability or education. The sense of being left behind, particularly with regard to sexuality, is usually accompanied by preoccupation with defects in their sexual attractiveness coming close to somatic delusion. This is at its most extreme and most puzzling where the girls are outstandingly beautiful and the boys especially attractive and charming. Their obsession with imagined defects leads directly into compulsive habits of food intake, exercising, health measures, and religious or quasi-religious ruminations. Their orientation to the adolescent community, and particularly to the sexual flamboyance, is' highly voyeurist, bitterly envious and despairing.

At the other pole are the youngsters who are left out of the healthy and necessary experimentation, whose pubertal masturbation chamber becomes socialized in a restricted sense to the subgroup of wildly promiscuous, drug and alcohol addicted and the thrill of criminality. Their recklessness smacks of despair and suicidal longings. When politicized or turned towards religious cults, they are fanatical. Because this over-the-top aspect does not bring ostracism but often admiration, it finds little to restrain it other than breakdown into physical or mental illness. Due to the lapse of parental influence they are rarely sent for therapy unless frank violence breaks out at home. This is not true of the Oblomovian luxuriators, whose frantic parents do send them, usually to little avail, for therapy. The dangers of venereal disease, of violence or of addiction deter them very little from the compulsive activities. Both groups of the left-behind from the joyous experimentation are riddled with tragedy.

And for both groups the way back from this brink is difficult, starting as it does in puberty with escalating alienation. As in all claustrum problems, the sexuality is so deeply rooted in unresolved pre-genitality and early emotional deprivation that the incapacity for emotional alliance, coupled with a deeply pessimistic view-of-the-world, makes it unlikely for them to have the kind of saving experience of being the object of a passionate love by a more healthy and mature person. Instead they easily fall prey to exploitation by dedicated older perverts, paraded as loving concern, whether homosexual or heterosexual.

146

Whether as therapists, parents, teachers or other representatives of the adult community, an understanding of the claustrophobic situation and its alienation from family life and the emotionality of human intimacy, may support efforts to "stand by". In order to be restrained from interference and yet hopeful, it seems necessary not only for parents to remember the child at his best earlier on, but to be able to see the desperation in the left-behind ones despite their bravado, contempt, provocativeness. A claustrum view highlights this shift in sense of identity, making it possible to recognise that they are different from earlier times, not only in their mental qualities, but also in the world they inhabit. One sees similar alterations in the refugee who cannot shake off his nightmare.

12   The Claustrum and the Perversions/ Addictions

The "revision" of Freud's "Three Essays on Sexuality" undertaken in *Sexual States of Mind* (1973) now requires some revision itself, in the light of subsequent digestion and implementation of Bion's work, some of which was reported in *Studies in Extended Metapsychology* and *The Apprehension of Beauty* (with Meg Harris Williams). But also the present explorations of the projective phenomenology of intrusive identification extends Melanie Klein's model of the mind, and requires special application to the perversions and addictions. The revision of Freud proposed in *Sexual States* was primarily a structural revision, taking into account splitting of self and objects, narcissistic identifications, struggle for control of the organ of consciousness (attention) and the war between creative and destructive tendencies seen, however, more at the level of self than of ego balancing life and death instincts.

This volume is devoted to this exploration of the projective phenomena accompanying intrusive identification, but they need a specific integration with Bion's theory of thinking with reference to the perversions and addictions. The aspect of his theory which is most significant for this purpose, and without which the idea of aesthetic conflict and its place in development and in the analytic process would not be possible, is Bion's new theory of affects, L (love), H (hate) and K (knowledge) as the emotional links of human relationships. Although it is ambiguous in his work, until, I think, *A Memoir of the Future,* this theory of plus and minus LHK completely shifts any idea of evil or destructiveness out of the realm of instinct, and therefore of constitution, genetics. Instead the emotionality, which is the heart of the matter of the life of the mind, of intimate and passionate relationships, and therefore of the growth of the personality (as distinct from the refinement of the adaptational carapace) is seen as struggling for expression in the face of an aversion to the turbulence (catastrophic change) which emotion entails. This gives a wider meaning to the concept of defense, for it implies also defense against emotion, not only against mental pain. Such a theory brings within the purview of analysis the whole puzzling region of defense against pleasure as well as pain, of what might be called the incapacity to enjoy one's happiness, dearth of joie de vivre.

Life in the claustrum has many pleasures, but what it certainly lacks is joie de vivre: happiness that comes from the experience of development, hopefulness that comes from direct – not second hand or once removed – contact with the beauty of the world. The head/breast has the pleasure of complacency, of elitism, of a delusion of security; the genital compartment has its erotic pleasure and "satisfaction", meaning exhaustion; the rectum offers variously the pleasures of sadism, masochism, power, wiliness, deception. In this model of the mind of extended metapsychology, that is, including Melanie Klein's geographic and Bion's epistemologic dimensions, the compartment of the claustrum entered by way of the anus, which means essentially from behind secretly, undergoes an alteration from its meaning in psychic reality. No longer the vital organ of the mother's mental economy served by the heroic aspects of the father's sexuality, it is found by the intruder to be an authoritarian world:

> 'Tis the same the whole world over;
> 'Tis the master who is right.
> 'Tis the boy who gets the beating;
> Serves the little bugger right!

The master of this compartment is the fecal penis, an object compounded of the paternal penis and of part of the self intruding into it which is utterly dedicated to minus LHK. Perhaps it is best defined as "cold" rather than "cruel" in its essence. Milton's Satan is hot, passionately envious and admiring. The serpent is cold, devious, calculating. It is the serpent, not Satan, that God curses, while with Satan he carries on an almost sporting contest for influence, as in the case of Job. Job's only complaint for being singled out for systematic suffering is the lack of direct communication. He'd gladly play his part in the game if only he were let know the rules. The rules of the game in the claustrum are unequivocal; it's the boy who gets the beating! And the game is hide and seek. It is "fun" despite the atmosphere of terror, as every nightmare is also a

150

horror film, as the rides in the fun fair are "thrilling". How delicate is the border between hunting or fishing for pleasure and blood sport.

Furthermore every intruder into this compartment of the claustrum is recruited for lieutenancy. He can be a hound as well as a hare, or he can be a hare disguised as a hound and a hound disguised as a hare. A most attractive game. One need not wonder at its popularity, from the point of view of "fun". But the fun is not its essence. This resides in the retreat from emotional links with other humans; the world of intimate, and therefore basically family, relationships. Seen from this additional vertex of the claustrum, it becomes apparent that in the midst of an addiction or a perverse phantasy or relationship, the person involved is not himself, he is "beside himself" with excitement, confusion as to the nature of the world, and deeply uncertain of the identity of any partner-in-crime. Perhaps the extraordinary evocative power of the crucifixion, leaving aside its spiritual meaning, is the crime of murdering the good baby – both the parents' new baby and the baby part of the person himself. For all sado-masochism seems to have this crime at its root, the minus LHK version of the passion in which a new baby is generated, its cold and exciting converse. The unforgiveable becomes forgiveable for, truly, they know not what they do.

In *Sexual States* the differentiation between habitual, dedicated and criminal perversity was suggested. The theory of the claustrum adds a new precision to this formulation. The habitual pervert would be the person whose sense of identity is not rooted in the part of the self ensconced in the claustrum. In analysis of such patients we have an opportunity to study the shifting back and forth of this control over the organ of attention in the ebb and flow of the transference. On the other hand the dedicated pervert is so rooted, but largely in the masochistic orientation, resisting recruitment to the staff of the claustrum with every means of deviousness he can muster but partici- pating fundamentally as the hare who must allow himself to be savaged periodically by the hound to placate its fury while less consciously indentifying also, in an accusatory way, with the mother who allows her baby to be violated to save herself (? "Mother Courage"). The criminal pervert has, however, been recruited and is following orders, with all the sanctimony of the nihilist and anarchist, political terrorist or inquisitor. Of the three subgroups he is truly "in despair" and his rehabilitation from the claustrum is barred, in his own mind, by the concreteness of the damage he has done in joining the ranks of the fecal penis. But even this may not be true, there may be no "mortal sin"; even the psycho-somatic executioner may reprieve. Regardless of the unworthiness of the motivation that leads to intrusion into the claustrum, once in there the "world" changes, the LH and K of intimate life disappears and is replaced by excitement shadowed by nameless dread. If punishment were necessary for forgiveness, these infantile parts have had their punishment, despite the "fun". I have suggested that the nameless dread is the possibility of insanity as thought disorder escalates and the delusional system of bizarre objects beckons, quite alluringly.

13   The Claustrum and Politics

It seems useless and self-deceptive to pretend that one can carry
on an activity at which others also labour without participating
in the communal aspect, for there is always a community. And
since there is a community there are problems of organization
and communication where the borderland between friendly and
hostile, communication and action, governing and ruling,
opposing and sabotaging becomes obscure. In everything I
have written some attention has been paid to the institutional
aspect of psycho-analysis in order to clarify to some extent the
organizational position from which I am intruding my thoughts
into the atmosphere. It is, naturally, an area in which I am
essentially ignorant, but I can comfort myself with the belief
that so are others, even alleged experts. So if I am an
embarrassment to my friends once again by making a fool of
myself, I remember Leonard Woolf's story about Hippolytes
standing on his head on the wedding banquet table because he
was too happy to care if he made a fool of himself. After all, in
the area of politics, who has showed himself more of a fool than
Plato?

A discussion of the implications of this imaginative conjecture of the claustrum for communal life follows directly from the
investigation of its operation in adolescence. Most of us were
still at this stage of life when we became involved in psycho-
analysis. It tends to persevere at least until the responsibility for
children and full responsibility for patients settles upon one. For
this reason, the format by which I have investigated adolescence
is valid here again: those who are able to participate in the
joyous experimentation with independence from analyst,
training committees and enforced supervision, and the others.
The Oblomovians keep their heads down and need not detain us
here, but all the other subcategories of claustrum dwellers find
representation, in psycho-analysis as in any organization; and
perhaps, if I am right about the ubiquity of this aspect of
personality structure, everyone's attitudes are subject to some
degree of influence by the claustrophobic view-of-the-world.

153

For most analysts the period of joyous adolescent experimentation is fairly promptly curtailed as the full responsibility entailed in independent analytic work begins to bend their spirits. And naturally they seek support, from carefully chosen supervisors, friends, cliques, groups. Because these are seldom truly intimate relationships, but at best friendly contractual ones, the political processes make themselves felt in self-deception and reduced sincerity, for the sake of preserving a spurious sense of harmony of thought and attitude. Perhaps it cannot be helped. Perhaps communal life would be hell, chaotic without these curtailments. But they creep into the consulting room as well. While I wish to address myself to this problem in the context of psycho-analysis, for this after all has been my major life experience of group life (I leave out eight years in the military as too rigid and primitive to be a learning experience), I think it has general application. Every group bears a strong resemblance to one or more compartments of the claustrum, which is another way of saying – in Bion's terms – that every work group tends towards basic assumption organization. I would pose the problems involved as: how to govern without ruling; how to communicate without acting; how to oppose without sabotaging; how to remain friendly when in disagreement?

To recapitulate briefly the characteristics of the compartments of the claustrum which particularly concern us here: the head/breast either confers elite status based on the delusion of clarity of insight and carries with it a sense of tenure, or it allows a sinecure of ease and comfort; the genital compartment promotes erotic preoccupation, either of the elect on the basis of supposed sexual attractiveness and potency, or a sense of disenfranchisement from these attributes; and the rectal compartment envelops the personality in an atmosphere of tyranny and submission, sado-masochism, pessimism and cynicism. Each compartment has its characteristic anxiety and corresponding idealization and complacency, depending on one's place in the hierarchy, for every compartment is essentially hierarchic.

With this compartmentalization in mind, let us try to elucidate the functions which need to be performed if an organization is to be governed in a manner consistent with its task. The main functions of the task of a psycho-analytical society, for instance, are to provide a place for scientific exchange and technical education, while also being able to represent the interests of the society vis à vis the community. In terms of the compartments of the claustrum, it must avoid conferring status, tenure, sinecures; it must avoid providing an ambience for erotic display and intrigue; it must discourage processes of tyranny or submission.

Such a statement, in all its banality, is an invitation to political solutions of the utopian stamp. The trouble perhaps lies in treating the organization as an organism, in referring to "it" as if there were mental qualities to be described. This is immediately the language of the basic assumption group, perhaps its most basic of basic assumptions. "Beach" is only a sign, a convenience, an agreed signifier for an innumerable collection of grains of sand. "Hive" is an organism: it can be named by symbol formation, and it can be filled with meaning as one investigates and comes to understand more of its organization. It is reasonable to assume that one hive is greatly similar to another. "Psycho-analytical Society" is a sign, designating a place: here are a collection of grains of psycho-analytical activity, with no inherent function or organization. For it to take on meaning, and therefore symbolic value, it can only do so as a summation of the activities of the individuals. Any table of organization will serve well or badly, depending on the participation of the individuals. But one thing it cannot become is a family. If it attempts that, it becomes a Basic Assumption Group Dependency.

The problem then — which if any group in the world is able to solve it should be psycho-analysts – is the problem of ethical individuality. But what in fact are the ethics of psycho-analysis? Even if psycho-analysis is an abstract thing-in-itself, which I confidently assert, it has no ethics. Only individuals can have ethics, and the model of the mind that I, and perhaps many psycho-analysts, embrace asserts that ethics are an emanation of the individual's internal objects. There can be no uniformity as there can be no homogeneity of individual history, regardless of degree of similarity, overlap. An individual's ethics are the values promulgated by his internal objects; their infringement is experienced in the unconscious as degrading to these objects —

essentially, as betrayal. In each individual these objects, like the self, are capable of learning from experience and need not be the same at thirty as they may be at sixty.

The ethics of the individual that would appear to be most consistent with the psycho-analytical method may be difficult to particularize at any specific moment of the therapy, but their broad outlines seem definable: to follow, not lead, in the search for the (unreachable) truth; to construct and preserve a setting in which this can take place; to enable the patient's evolution without goals; to search for meaning and not to exert moral judgment on behaviour; to be prepared for personal sacrifice in the pursuit of these aims, while not imposing these sacrifices on others; to restrict one's influence on the patient to the clarity shed by communication and not through actions; to speak truthfully, as reflected in both words and music.

It is probably impossible for an individual to behave in the contractual atmosphere of a work group with the same ethics as he may be able to achieve in the intimate climate of a good analysis. But he can possibly avoid degradation, without imposing his individual ethics on others. If we return to the aspects of the compartmentalization and hierarchic world of claustrophobic mentality, we might be able to define these characteristic pitfalls of degradation, and to a) guard against accepting the status of an expert, by preserving the understanding that in this field there is no knowledge, only opinion based on experience; b) refuse the sinecure conferred by overcharging on the basis of the supposed high opinion of one's colleagues; c) be alert to the intensity of the erotic charge in the analytic situation, supervision and exhibition of one's work; d) refuse participation in group functions which are not enabling but restrictive, punitive, disciplinary; e) avoid attributing failures to the patient rather than to one's own work or the limitations of psycho-analysis; f) avoid selecting patients, for this leads inevitably to exploitation of junior colleagues by referring difficult, unattractive and poorly paying patients to them; g) do your share of the society's dirty work, but no more, lest you be rewarded with status difficult to refuse politely; h) get thrown out when the atmosphere of the society has become too degrading even for tacit participation, without being schismatic.

These seem to me to be tenable principles for participation in a community without degradation, and may therefore be considered as an anti-political position. It is in keeping with the basic ethic of the just man, to mind one's business and mind it well. Now considerations of the claustrum suggest that there are two compartments which are eminently political in their orientation: the Proustian aspect of the head/breast and the recruited-to-lieutenancy one in the rectum. The former manifest a drive for status that is easily gratified by the hierarchic structure, and the latter a greed for power where enabling has been replaced by restrictive practices. The heroes-of-the-resistance in the rectum are the schismatic agitators whose deviousness is matched by their zeal and self-righteousness. It is probably inevitable that any group which forms with a work-group intention and a certain revolutionary enthusiasm should grow "old", not only in the sense of the ageing of its founders, but with its growth in membership — its increasing popularity and its waxing respectability. With this ageing the shift towards basic assumption orientation progresses with the size of the rule book and its tacit belief in political methods. It is natural that in the more claustrophobic, organizationally serious and ambitious atmosphere the more charismatic and the party work-horses, should rise to the top. Rebellions by the heroes-of-the-resistance produce only palace revolutions which change nothing of the essentially political atmosphere. This is the "neighbour's smoke" that tells you it is time to "move on". It may seem a lonely business to act justly, but not really. There is a tacit camaraderie amongst the workers.

Addendum: *Macbeth's Equivocation, Shakespeare's Ambiguity*
Meg Harris-Williams

(i) Equivocation versus Ambiguity

Shakespeare became interested in the concept of equivocation in the gravedigger scene in *Hamlet*, in the context of covering-up versus unearthing truth. In *Macbeth* he pursues it relentlessly in a way which probably established its modern meaning of using one idea, image or word to disguise another, leading by its very nature to the establishment of a type of sub-language or social jargon; it is 'the fiend/That lies like truth'. This play equivocates on the concepts of 'success' 'growth' and 'safety', which all cover over an underlying meaning of death or destruction; 'taking off' means 'murdered' just as in modern military jargon 'taking out' means 'destroy'. Equivocation is thus in complete contrast to poetic ambiguity, which includes more than the double meaning of words and phrases alone; it is a means of capturing meaning between the lines of a dual image or character or dramatic event — between any of the formal ingredients of a play, presented in such a way as to evoke echoes and parallels between them; meaning is evoked, rather than pinned down reductively. Key images, themes, and linguistic echoes in a play which contribute to its organic structure belong to the realms of ambiguity — such as, in this play, the organising image of the new-born babe: on this focusses the concept of living-out the future as opposed to controlling the future (see C. Brooks on 'The Naked Babe' and M. M. Mahood on 'Macbeth's Wordplay'). Equivocation is a means of self-deception, whether it occurs in the form of the blatant cynicism of Lady Macbeth, or in Macbeth's confused haze — trying to hide his 'deed' from his 'self', his 'hand' from his 'eye', etc. Ambiguity, on the other hand, is the fundamental artistic means of exploration and discovery, the means of self-analysis; instead of covering-up, it reveals the mystery of some emotional predicament.

In *Macbeth* Shakespeare undertakes the difficult task of approaching poetically the most unpoetical of subjects; for the Romantic dictum that it is much easier to portray vividly a character in hell than one in heaven only applies when the character is half in and half out — in a state of conflict in an ambiguous situation, like Hamlet. The subject of Macbeth — or the Macbeths — in hell is innately boring and antipathetic, and Shakespeare has to approach their claustrum of equivocation from different angles, including means of entry and exit, is such a way that we can actually experience the meaning of meaninglessness, as an everyday condition which exists beyond the confines of hellfire and fairytale witches. One of the structural types of ambiguity which enables him to do this' is the separation of the hero into two components, the characters of Macbeth and Lady Macbeth, as a means of showing clearly the perversion of femininity; likewise they are contrasted with the Macduff family in a way which suggests split aspects of the same personality. Another of the playwright's devices is the linguistic interweaving of the witch-values with society's respectable codes of honour and success, so that Macbeth never seems to us to be a monster or 'hell-kite' (as his contemporaries claim), but rather, a victim of his own equivocation — the easy way out of a mental conflict — whose nightmare consequences are perhaps surprising. Lady Macbeth and her husband believe they know what they are doing when they daringly eschew their childish catechisms about good and evil and decide to seize the System by the horns and make it work for them, in a spirit of modern opportunism. The point of gaining the Crown — the 'golden round', the 'imperial theme' — is to become immune from fate and chance, from contradictions without and within; possession of the crown shall

> to all our nights and days to come
> Give solely sovereign sway and masterdom.(I.v.69 – 70)

It derives from belief in a false masculinity which is omniscient and omnipotent, in predetermined control of events and in league with a perverse femininity which traps and enslaves or kills. The Macbeths fall easy prey to the witches since they already believe in a hierarchy of spirits who 'know all mortal consequence' and serve hidden 'masters', a version of Big Brother; through identifying with the witch-mind, they believe they can become Big Brother in their own realm. This is what prevents them from having any real, developing future — from having spiritual 'heirs' to their mental kingdom, children of the imagination resulting from a creative male and female union. It is the mind more than the body which becomes sterile and heirless. Yet the sense of emptiness which ensues immediately after the first murder can only be interpreted by them in terms of having failed to get complete control of the crown: hence the repetitive sequence of murders, and the mind's revenge of hallucination and madness ⌐— features of imprisonment in the claustrum.

During the Renaissance, hell came to be envisaged in English literature as a state of mind rather than a place: a state characterised by restless activity glossing over underlying despair and self-imprisonment; in the words of Milton's Satan,

'Which way I fly am hell; myself am hell' (*Paradise Lost*, IV.75).

The flight is from the meaninglessness of an existence which, while imprisoning, provides no containment for the soul — the ever-deepening abyss of 'bottomless perdition' (in modern terms, the conviction of being worked-over, 'overworked' by The System). Satan is, initially at least, the poet of his own predicament, before the pressures of leadership make him a slave to his own jargon. But in *Macbeth*, the hero's degradation is expressed dramatically rather than lyrically, through the structure and language of the entire play. Indeed Macbeth is doomed to lose the faculty for self-expression — though this begins to return from the moment when he learns to 'begin to doubt the equivocation of the fiend/That lies like truth'. Shakespeare uses for a backdrop the traditional iconography of hell in its gaudiest and goriest colours — the unnatural palls of darkness in daytime, bloodsmoked haze, owls shrieking, horses eating one another, etc. — all issuing from the witches' cauldron with its mess of dismembered, poisonous ingredients, to illuminate the 'primrose way to the everlasting bonfire'. There is almost a sense of caricature about these fairytale 'painted devils' — which Lady Macbeth scorns as being feared by 'the eye of childhood' (II.ii.53). But the sinister quality of the play derives from the way the flamboyant iconography of the primrose path is translated into a history of the degeneration of thought processes within the mind of the hero (and heroine), beginning with the bloodsmoked haze which finds its spiritual counterpart in the fuzz of mindless equivocations. Shakespeare uses dramatic and poetic ambiguity to penetrate the fuzz of equivocation and expose the real outcome for Macbeth of his reliance on the witches — the loss of his ability to experience life as meaningful.

The first act of the play shows us a society in the throes of wrecking itself through civil wars, hence not surprisingly dominated by the spirit of the witches on their blasted heath brewing malignant troubles from mutilated and faecal ingredients. But the key feature of their brew is not that it is evil but that it is equivocal:

Fair is foul and foul is fair
Hover through the fog and filthy air. (I.i. 11 – 12).

Their brew is a 'double' one ('double double toil and trouble') whose fair appearance hides its inner or essential foulness. The witches never explicitly command Macbeth to murder; they direct him towards 'the crown', 'success' or 'knowledge of the future' which Shakespeare shows us to be inherently murderous goals, though not antagonistic to society's values but in line with its basic assumptions. In fact the witch-values are generated by society, though they only become overtly hellish or destructive during unstable times, and Macbeth becomes their victim and instrument not owing to his innate evil but owing to his weak-mindedness. As Milton's Samson says, 'All wickedness is weakness'. Macbeth is, in everyone's eyes, a decent fellow — according to his wife, 'full o' th' milk of human kindness' (I.v.17) — but he cannot think through the temptations facing him. He slips into the primrose path to perdition partly owing to identification with the evil quality of the witch-mind (its perverted femininity, pressed on him by his wife), but more crucially, owing to identification with its *methods*, of thought-smothering equivocation. And Shakespeare demonstrates in the first act how these modes of un-thinking dominate society's creation of its heroes. Macbeth will vanquish one traitor — the Thane of Cawdor — only in order to fill his position himself and to complete its treachery successfully, as far as the 'crown' of ambition. Dramatic irony makes this seem an inevitable process: thus Macbeth engages Cawdor by 'confronting him with self-comparisons'; then Duncan decides to offer him Cawdor's position with the words 'What he hath lost, noble Macbeth hath won' (echoing the witches' phrase 'When the battle's lost and won'); finally Macbeth enters the king's presence at the point when he is lamenting that he misplaced his 'absolute trust' in Cawdor because there was no way of seeing 'the mind's construction in the face'; by straightway transferring this 'absolute trust' to his new hero, Duncan seems to put the seal of approval on his rumbling treachery. Thus the pilot whom the witches say they 'shipwrecked' on his way 'homeward' refers in the context of the play back to Cawdor who 'laboured in his country's wreck', and forward to Macbeth whom they are waiting to wreck, before he can arrive at his spirit's 'home' after the confusion of the battle. These are all functions of Shakespeare's ambiguity. As a soldier, Macbeth receives rapturous praise as 'Bellona's bridegroom', 'valour's minion', for creating 'strange images of death' and 'unseaming' his enemies 'from the nave to the chops', in a manner parallelling the witches filling their cauldron; then society's own equivocations in which 'foul is fair' make it but a small step for him to carry on completing the role of the successful one, founded on bloody deeds; such deeds have become an inbuilt feature of the path to 'success'.

'They met me in the day of success', Macbeth tells his wife in his letter introducing the witches. The witches hailed him according to a progressive pattern in promotion: Glamis — Cawdor — King; and each time Macbeth is hailed by his new titles, following this pattern or its first stages, he seems further bound to the witch-mind as the source of what are equivocally known as 'truths':

> Two truths are told,
> As happy prologues to the swelling act
> Of the imperial theme ...
> This supernatural soliciting
> Cannot be ill; cannot be good:
> If ill, why has it given me earnest of success,
> Commencing in a truth? I am Thane of Cawdor:
> If good, why do I yield to that suggestion

> Whose horrid image doth unfix my hair ...
> My thought, whose murther yet is but fantastical,
> Shakes so my single state of man,
> That function is smother'd in surmise,
> And nothing is, but what is not. (I.iii1127 – 42)

The language of pregnancy and birth, the 'swelling act', is used to disguise the 'horrid image' of murder — presented ambiguously as murdering in thought, and the murder of thought itself. The progression of these equivocal 'truths' (a rhythmic balance between 'ill' and 'good') mounts to an automatic culmination in murder. It is a goal which Macbeth prefers to find 'fantastical', and allows to be 'smothered' over again by reverting to cryptic equivocation, again based on the idea of pregnancy — 'And nothing is but what is not'. In this way Macbeth fails to confront the implications of the witches' sinister progression; and with each failure, Shakespeare shows how his hero submits further to the trap which is closing in on him, with his mind befogged by 'surmise'. By interdigitating the values of the court and the cauldron, in an ambiguous juxtaposition, Shakespeare shows how Macbeth becomes entrammelled in a special relationship with the king whose sinister undertone means succession/success by replacement/murder, or 'swelling' growth by feeding on the host's blood. This is the 'foul' side of the 'fair' equivocation about hierarchical success which is acquiesced in by everyone, not Macbeth alone, and which makes respectable society vulnerable to the witch-values. It is associated with the medieval idea of the body politic, seeing the state as an organism with its members growing on or out of each other, feeding one another through bloodlinks which are supposed to represent 'absolute trust' or intimacy, and all focussed on the king. Hence the conventional jargon after his murder is discovered: 'The wine of life is drawn', 'the life o' th' building', etc. (II.iii.69 – 96). The incipient instability, treachery and bloodthirstiness of this model were described by Shakespeare in *Richard II*. Here in *Macbeth*, the naive and saintly Duncan says he intends to 'plant' Macbeth and make him 'full of growing' (also Banquo); meanwhile he receives Macbeth's formal compliments as a 'banquet' on which he 'feeds'; their relationship seems so special that he desires to 'bind' Macbeth to him, in an ominously ambiguous way, saying: 'More is thy due than more than all can pay'. The language of compliment has a sinister literalness which Shakespeare shows is not merely accidental but somehow conveys the unthinking expectations of society's basic assumptions. Thus it is that the 'horrid image' of the king's murder (always cloaked in equivocation) comes to present itself to Macbeth as though it were — as Bradley said — 'an appalling duty'.

In the first act therefore, the trap is laid for Macbeth as the hero-cum-victim on his way homeward. Gradually the pressure of hidden expectations, coupled with the speed of events, begin to overtake him. He tries to fall back on the soldier's maxim — 'Time and the hour runs through the roughest day' — hoping that he will not have to make any active decision, any more than he did on the battlefield: 'If Chance will have me king, why, Chance may crown me/Without my stir'. Goodnatured passivity and not being too much in the limelight may have always saved him in the past from any temptations to criminality. Indeed, we feel that had it not been for Lady Macbeth (the guardian of Macbeth's home), and for society's mad rush which plays into her hands, Macbeth would probably have escaped through inertia, and kept his reputation for nobility.

(ii) Entry to the Claustrum

It is the figure of Lady Macbeth which enables Shakespeare to probe the full implications of the state of mind exemplified in Macbeth. Although the air is thick with equivocation, confusion and murderous potential after the fighting, it is she who ensures that his downward course of 'success' is irrevocably precipitated into action ('screwed' to the 'sticking place' in her phrase). In another poetic juxtaposition, Shakespeare suddenly transfers king, family, courtiers and generals that very night to the confines of Lady Macbeth's castle. It is done with lightning speed and a sense of frantic urgency, with messengers 'almost dead for breath' and the king trying to outride Macbeth — whose 'great love, sharp as his spur' nonetheless makes him win the race. Those who do not make it to the castle that night are knocking at the gate before dawn the next morning — to be

165

welcomed all by the 'devil-porter' as 'equivocators' on their way to the 'everlasting bonfire'. The castle is presented as a feminine enclosure: as when Lady Macbeth (referring to the breathless messenger who brings the 'great news' of Duncan's arrival) says:

> The raven himself is hoarse
> That croaks the fatal entrance of Duncan
> Under my battlements. (I.v.38 – 40)

On the outside, she and her castle appear 'fair': an idyllic haven or 'cradle' in which 'temple-haunting martlets' may nest (I.vi.4), a place of security and nurture for infant souls. In this context, Duncan is described as if he were a satisfied infant put to sleep, retiring to bed 'shut up/In measureless content', surrounded by other images of childhood, including his young sons; even his bodyguards are mere children, easily seduced and slaughtered. But the castle is a place of equivocation, an extension of the fairytale witches' cauldron, a murderous trap. It comes to symbolise Lady Macbeth's explicitly perverted femininity, which has been emptied of the milk of human kindness and filled with 'gall' or evil spirits:

> Come, you Spirits
> That tend on mortal thoughts, unsex me here,
> And fill me, from the crown to the toe, top-full
> Of direst cruelty! make thick my blood,
> Stop up th'access and passage to remorse; ...
> Come to my woman's breasts,
> And take my milk for gall, you murth'ring ministers,
> Wherever in your sightless substances
> You wait on Nature's mischief! Come, thick Night,
> And pall thee in the dunnest smoke of Hell,
> That my keen knife see not the wound it makes,
> Nor Heaven peep through the blanket of the dark,
> To cry, "Hold, hold!" (I.v.40 – 54)

Her language invokes the bloodsmoked haze associated with the witches and with Macbeth's prowess on the battlefield ('Unsex ... from crown to toe' echoing 'unseam ... from nave to chops').

It is literally an unsexing, a perversion of femininity (not an ambiguous extension of it): focussing on the body as a claustrophobic trap with its passages of communication stopped up, only penetrable by wounding, and with the idea of masculinity (her husband) present only in the form of her 'knife', a mere mechanical instrument of destruction. This is her castle, her 'battlements', in which she is about to receive Duncan with his saintly and childlike connotations — himself like an infant peeping throught the blanket, whose glance encounters no responding ray of sight from 'sightless substances' and their 'murthering ministers'.

Lady Macbeth's imagery finds its counterpart of ambiguity in Macbeth's next soliloquy, his first genuine attempt to ask himself what he really feels about the murder, now that his wife has confronted him with its execution and both he and Duncan are placed together under her roof. Macbeth has to leave the supper table early in order to have even the shortest space of time alone in which to consider his decision. At first, his ability to think is hampered by the prevailing fuzz of equivocation, with its punning upon the concepts of 'sequence' 'cease' and 'success'.

> If it were done, when 'tis done, then 'twere well
> It were done quickly: if th'assassination
> Could trammel up the consequence, and catch
> With his surcease success; that but this blow
> Might be the be-all and the end-all — here,
> But here, upon this bank and shoal of time,
> We'd jump the life to come. (I.vii. 1 – 7)

Ostensibly Macbeth is considering the 'consequences' of both eternal and then earthly judgement and retribution, in this speech. But the significant message, relayed through poetry rather than argument, is that for him 'success' is a condition with no consequence in the sense of no future: would Duncan's 'surcease' constitute a 'be-all and an end-all' also for Macbeth himself, a cessation of life's trials at one 'blow'? The foul fact of murder seems a mere formality ('done — done — done'), slithered over through the sounds of the wordplay, as if it were itself a mere noise: 'assassination — consequence —surcease —

success', the single blow of success. And the fair face which covers it is, for Macbeth, a state of finite security, an escapist longing, more passive than Lady Macbeth's desire to control and command others: it is a conflict-free haven, a succession free from consequences of any kind, not merely retributive; in effect a type of death (as in Keats's 'cease upon the midnight with no pain'). After the murder, he will say of Duncan: 'After life's fitful fever he sleeps well'. But even before the murder, for Macbeth in his deep depression, life is already a fitful fever, and the imagery indicates his envy of the sleeping and the dead. It is not only the afterlife of eternity but his own future life which he would like to successfully cease, marooned upon a sandbank and removed from the flux of existence. This would be his goal in possessing the crown. If one blow could make him king in this sense, being-all and ending-all, he would do it.

It is not until Macbeth considers Duncan himself, in the light of his own relation to him (which is at the moment a paternal one — being his host) that he comes into contact with his own emotional core, and seems to wake up for the first time in the play:

> Besides, this Duncan
> Hath borne his faculties so meek, hath been
> So clear in his great office, that his virtues
> Will plead like angels, trumpet-tongu'd, against
> The deep damnation of his taking-off;
> And Pity, like a naked new-born babe,
> Striding the blast, or heaven's Cherubim, hors'd
> Upon the sightless couriers of the air,
> Shall blow the horrid deed in every eye,
> That tears shall drown the wind. — I have no spur
> To prick the sides of my intent, but only
> Vaulting ambition, which o'erleaps itself
> And falls on th'other — (I.vii.16 – 28)
>   (*Enter* Lady Macbeth)

'Taking off', a euphemism for destroy (as in 'takes your enemy off', II.i.104), is associated with 'jumping' the life to come; but here it also, ambiguously, becomes a metaphor for achieving a spiritual life, focussed on the new-born babe who is surrounded by angels ('trumpet-tongu'd' so able to speak meaningfully) and riding the horses of the winds (elemental couriers and carriers of passion). Duncan becomes the new-born babe Pity, guarded by the cherubim (angels of spiritual knowledge); and in turn this becomes a representation of Macbeth's own soul, newly-born because newly seen. In this symbolic cloud-formation (illustrated by Blake) 'sightless couriers' direct their ray of feeling into 'every eye', thus contrasting with Lady Macbeth's 'sightless ministers' who inhabit the witch-like fog of equivocation, the blanket of the dark, which can be pierced only with knives not sight; it contrasts also with the artificially cocooned 'shoal of time' in its unfeeling limbo. The poetry of this passage therefore conveys a process of perception in Macbeth, achieved by opening up a means of internal communication — the 'access to Remorse' whose passage Lady Macbeth had vowed to stop up. As a visual expression of emotional reality it is, potentially, Macbeth's strongest defence so far against committing the murder.

But Macbeth is unable to translate the feeling which he has suddenly discovered into terms of active argument; he is still a novice in the field of thinking. He immediately falls back into a passive state of non-responsibility: 'I have no spur/To prick the sides of my intent' — that is, nothing is goading him onwards, so there is no need for him to proceed; events can sort themselves out without his 'stir' (as he said earlier). His own horse of 'ambition' seems out-matched by the heavenly ones and he is content to let them win the course — but without making the crucial step of personal commitment. He is therefore doubly vulnerable when Lady Macbeth enters, precisely on cue, and shows herself to be the 'spur' which Macbeth hoped he lacked. During the ensuing section of dialogue, Macbeth becomes ensnared helplessly in her trap. He does not attempt to convey any of the force of the feeling from the soliloquy, but instead argues lamely that he does not want to lose the 'golden opinions' he has just won 'from all sorts of people'; he would like to wear these for a while 'in their newest gloss,/Not cast aside so soon'. Macbeth was already feeling uncomfortable (albeit flattered) by being 'dressed in borrowed robes' — loaded with titular honours and pressed into a false intimacy with the king; yet they suited his ambition, and he had hoped they would appease his ambitious 'partner of greatness', his wife (I.v.11). The theme of false clothing which does not express the inner man is used by Shakespeare throughout the play in association with the theme of equivocation. For Lady Macbeth it is the externalities which make the man, rather than vice versa; she retaliates furiously: 'Was the hope drunk,/ Wherein you dress'd yourself?' The golden crown is the only clothing worth having since it overrides any number of golden opinions; she is not interested in appearance as a means of social facilitation but only in the power which it denotes, and as she asks uncomprehendingly in her later sleepwalking: 'What need we fear who knows it, when none can call our power to accompt?'

Macbeth is doomed, but he makes one final heroic attempt to save himself from the degradation which she is thrusting upon him, with the words:

> Pry'thee, peace.
> I dare do all that may become a man;
> Who dares do more, is none.

The words are few but meaningful, particularly in the wider context of the play's imagery. He implies his own definition of integrity and manliness is as something distinct from the gloss of other people's opinions and from power: some deeds are 'becoming' and some are not, but their measure is internally not externally taken. But Lady Macbeth, faced with this unexpected rebellion, rounds on her 'beast' of a husband savagely with her own definition of manhood as one who dares to 'do' what he phantasizes, rather than being 'unmade' by it; the occasion, opportunistically seized, becomes the man:

> When you durst do it, then you were a man;
> And, to be more than what you were, you would
> Be so much more the man. Nor time, nor place,
> Did then adhere, and yet you would make both:
> They have made themselves, and that their fitness now
> Does unmake you.

Lady Macbeth had claimed she would vanquish her husband through the 'valour of her tongue'; but what ultimately overpowers him is not her direct chastisement. Rather, it is her instinctive recognition of his Achilles' heel, which she earlier called the 'milk of human kindness', and which she now interprets in terms of the new-born babe of his soliloquy:

> I have given suck, and know
> How tender 'tis to love the babe that milks me:
> I would, while it was smiling in my face,
> Have pluck'd my nipple from his boneless gums,
> And dash'd the brains out, had I so sworn
> As you have done to this.

The image of the babe lay at the heart of his temporary rebellion against her, resulting in the definition of manhood which she found so infuriating. Macbeth is at his most vulnerable at the moment when he begins to think for himself; his capacity for thinking is itself new-born and undeveloped, and his habitual passivity prevents him from protecting it. Lady Macbeth's brazen image of infanticide is taken by him (as she intended) as an attack on his own infant soul, her knife cutting through his blanket of equivocation. He feels paralysed, in effect by terror, owing to what he calls her 'undaunted mettle', her pseudomasculinity. Using the language of admiration — 'bring forth men-children only!' — he acknowledges his subservience to her, as a witch in woman's clothing, and submits to being recruited as her agent. In this way, Shakespeare uses dramatic irony and poetic ambiguity to pursue to the utmost the implications of Macbeth's wavering condition — the origins of the 'mind diseased' which might otherwise have remained obscured by equivocation's shadowy cloak.

(iii) Life in the Claustrum

Macbeth carries out the murder in a hallucinated state, as though drugged, led by the dagger in mid-air: 'I go, and it is done'. From this point he is no longer himself, has no internal contact, but feels a mere agent or vehicle of the witch-mind: 'To know my deed, 'twere best not know myself' (II.ii.72). He has allowed his 'hand' to become Lady Macbeth's 'knife', and tries to carry out the splitting of self from deed, eye from hand, which he had postulated earlier as a means of defence ('the eye wink at the hand'), as if not knowing or seeing what he was doing could somehow detach him from the consequences of 'success'. His most sincere comment in public during the commotion after the murder is discovered is, ''Twas a rough night' — recalling the vain hope that the unpleasant feeling might pass, just as 'Time and the hour runs through the roughest day'. Indeed in his disturbed state shortly after the murder he is still able to express disjointedly but poetically his awareness of the damage his 'hand' has inflicted on his inner world:

> this my hand will
> The multitudinous seas incarnadine,
> Making the green one red. (II.ii.60 – 2)

The variety of life (conveyed by the polysyllabic 'multitudinous') is permeated in every aspect by the matching 'incarnadine'; while the monosyllabic 'this my hand' is confirmed by 'green one red' (recalling the 'done — done — done' echoed throughout the play). Instead of refuge on a sandbank from the seas of eternity, the hand which he would like to disown reduces his entire world to a fatal monotony. Voices cry to him that 'Macbeth hath murdered Sleep — the innocent sleep', the source of fruitful dreaming. He hears enough from within to confirm the destructive significance of the murder to himself, but thereafter is merely hounded by the symptoms — the 'terrible dreams', hallucinations, nameless dread, envy of the dead and obsession with safety:

> Better be with the dead,
> Whom we, to gain our peace, have sent to peace,
> Than on the torture of the mind to lie
> In restless ecstacy. (III.ii.19 – 22)

Having made his mind a bed of torture he has to lie on it. Lady Macbeth had taunted him to 'screw his courage to the sticking-place', in Duncan's body; now he can no longer waver, but finds himself stuck in a repetitive sequence seeking further sticking-places for his 'fear':

> To be thus is nothing, but to be safely thus:
> Our fears in Banquo
> Stick deep, and in his royalty of nature

Reigns that which would be fear'd: 'Tis much he dares;
And, to that dauntless temper of his mind,
He hath a wisdom that doth guide his valour
To act in safety. (III.i.47 – 53)

Only now does Macbeth become obsessed with his lack of heirs
— the 'barren sceptre in his gripe'. As Shakespeare's imagery
showed, the murder of Duncan had for the Macbeths the
psychological meaning of infanticide, including the sense of the
murder of thought and 'of' mind-restoring sleep: stifling all'
possibility of creativity in their relationship, and the potential of
a developing future. In this sense, he has indeed no heirs; yet
Macbeth himself does not recognise this, and the 'defilement' of
his mind has a different meaning for him: 'For Banquo's issue
have I fil'd my mind ... To make them kings, the seed of
Banquo kings!' Banquo's heirs seem to be the evidence of his
innate 'royalty' and 'wisdom' — yet already, these concepts
have come to have a debased meaning, contingent on knowing
how to 'act in safety'. A real king is a 'safe' one, who makes sure
he has heirs — not in the sense of a developing future, but in the
sense of control of the future; his heirs are his bodyguard, the
guarantee of safety at the price of a little defilement. Macbeth is
persecuted not by remorse, or even guilt (at this stage), but by
the consumerist suspicion that he has been tricked into a false
kingship; he has paid the asking price and delivered his 'eternal
jewel' to 'the common Enemy of man', but has been returned
faulty goods, with defective safety features and no guarantee.

His reign of terror therefore begins with the character of a
massive clean-up operation, designed to rectify his position
which is 'unsafe the while'. And this time there will be no
defilement, no paying over the odds; it will be a clean job. For
the ideals of safety and of cleanliness are concurrent, and both
euphemisms for murder, in terms of the phantasy that the court
must not become too dirty with the king's enemies. Macbeth
now shrinks from using his own sullied hands. In order to
separate 'eye' from 'hand' even further, he hires three
murderers to dispose of Banquo and his son Fleance in the naive
belief that he can abnegate responsibility: then later when
Banquo's ghost appears to him he hastily excuses himself with,
'Thou canst not say, I did it'. It is also necessary to his phantasy

that the murderers should say they are committing the crime on their own behalf, as injured parties like himself. Using the language of the ideological tyrant, Macbeth hectors them about how Banquo is their hated enemy who has 'bowed them to the grave and beggared them for ever'; not only must they kill him, but they must *want* to kill him, for the good of the state and for love of the king — a deed 'whose execution takes your enemy off' and 'grapples you to the heart and love of us' (III,i.104 – 5). The language of political manipulation is based on the devaluation of concepts such as 'growth', 'love' and 'freedom'. He uses arguments not unlike those which Lady Macbeth had used on him; and they reply, as he did: 'We are men, my Liege' — which calls forth Macbeth's 'catalogue' of dog-men:

Ay, in the catalogue ye go for men;
As hounds, and greyhounds, mongrels, spaniels, curs,
Shoughs, water-rugs, and demi-wolves, are clept
All by the name of dogs: (III.91 – 4)

Macbeth claims that the murder would elevate them from 'the worst rank of manhood'; but unlike him, they have at least the virtue that they claim to be no more than hit-men, careless of their own lives, willing to carry out their ruler's dirty orders. In bullying them until they acquiesce in his phantasy of cleanliness and sanctimony, Macbeth sinks to a position far lower then theirs. Equivocation has for him become a means of systematically degrading others, rather than merely something to hide himself behind.

The pursuit of 'safety' thus takes on the characteristics of political ideology and false art or faecal obsessionality. Macbeth wants his crown — his position in the hierarchy — to be safe, clean, perfect. He demands 'a clearness' in the murder of Banquo, leaving 'no rubs or botches in the work'; and on hearing that Fleance has escaped, he feels trapped by this flaw in the perfection of the marble which constitutes himself:

Then comes my fit again: I had else been perfect;
Whole as the marble, founded as the rock,
As broad and general as the casing air;
But now, I am cabin'd, cribb'd, confin'd, bound in
To saucy doubts and fears. — But Banquo's safe?
(III.iv.19 – 24)

Banquo's ghost returns in the form of a vengeful hallucination, threatening not the easy revenge of death (a type of safety and perfection) but the nightmare terror of dispossession: squeezing Macbeth from his place at the table, so that — he believes — there is nowhere for him to sit. Banquo is 'safe' in the sense of dead, but not in the sense of his image having been 'taken off' or erased. Instead of Banquo's removal, it is Macbeth who is first squeezed ('cabin'd, cribb'd, confin'd') then evacuated into non-existence. Macbeth is prey to his own equivocation as the ghost comes and goes several times, responding to his invitation to 'our dear friend Banquo — would he were present'. Whenever it appears, Macbeth finds that his seat (the place of his own crown) is blocked by the gory faecal 'crown' of Banquo's mutilated corpse — the 'twenty mortal murthers on his crown' caused by 'twenty trenched gashes in his head'. The solidity of this apparition literally 'pushes' Macbeth 'from his stool'. It is poetic justice with a vengeance. Shakespeare clarifies the link between the 'doing' (of murder — in this play's euphemistic shorthand) and defaecation, through the ambiguity of Lady Macbeth's rebuke: 'When all's done, you look but on a stool'. For a short while, in fact, Macbeth rises above his fear, wondering at the metaphysical aspect of the situation.

> the time has been,
> That, when the brains were out, the man would die,
> And there an end; but now, they rise again,
> With twenty mortal murthers on their crowns,
> And push us from our stools. This is more strange
> Than such a murther is ... (III.iv.77 – 82)

The 'strangeness' of this false intimacy with the dead Banquo is Shakespeare's poetic correlative to his false intimacy with the dead Duncan; it presents the true character of his usurpation and 'success', and for a moment Macbeth is perplexed, since he had not (any more than his wife) imagined the nature of 'even-handed justice' (retribution) as something arising out of his own consciousness. They knew there was such a thing as 'remorse', which could be 'stopped up', but not that this very constipation would conjure up a world of delusion. Lady Macbeth is the first to see the approach of madness, looking at her husband after

Duncans's murder and then with Banquo's ghost; but her only defence is to stop 'thinking' about the 'deeds' for 'it will make us mad' (II.ii.33); in fact the inability to think is what precipitates her madness. Her 'thoughts' have indeed 'died/With them they think on' (III.ii.10).

Macbeth's 'wonder' at this strangenes is transient, 'like a summer's cloud', since he like his wife has no means of investigating its meaning, with his internal communication blocked. He is driven to the witches, like a heroine addict to the needle, for further injections of what he knows is bad for him ('damned all those that trust them'), in search of the pseudo-knowledge which will give him a delusory protection from the future:

> for now I am bent to know,
> By the worst means, the worst. For mine own good,
> All causes shall give way: I am in blood
> Stepp'd in so far, that, should I wade no more,
> Returning were as tedious as go o'er.
> Strange things I have in head, that will to hand,
> Which must be acted, ere they may be scann'd.
> (III.iv.133 – 9)

Macbeth's mode of argument has now become a string of trite slogans rationalised under the heading of political necessity, as the only courageous procedure in difficult times. He equivocates on the word 'worst', as though he were heroically facing up to the most painful facts — disguising what is really entailed by 'the worst means'; he pretends to be taking unpleasant procedures 'for his own good' — disguising the nature of the 'causes which give way'; the image of the river of blood (classical political rhetoric) is used to flow over the significance of this 'going o'er' — that is, continuing to commit murders — also to disguise the impossibility of 'returning'; he is prepared to assume the 'tedious' burden. Finally, the 'strange things' in his head (like the 'strange images of death' from the battlefield), which we have just seen exemplified in the scene with Banquo's ghost, are masqueraded as ideas which insist upon realisation — they 'will to hand', 'must be acted': a coming-to-birth metaphor which is again a euphemism for murder. Through this pseudologicality, Macbeth perpetrates the lie-in-the-soul that he is prepared to sacrifice his comfort in the interests of political necessity. Until those uncomfortable 'things' in his head have been 'acted', he cannot 'scan' the information contained in them and get an overview for the state's efficient functioning — reliable predictions of the course things will and must take in the future.

This is the state of mind in which Macbeth pays a further visit to the witches. His wife is no further use in this scanning-through-action (in fact he never speaks to her again in the play); he needs access to the central computer. The witches obligingly respond, according to his desire to be goaded onwards. They show him Banquo's lines of descendants, which fuels Macbeth with the specific determination to murder instantly and automatically all those to hand who remind him that he has a barren sceptre in his grip, an unsafe crown:

> From this moment,
> The very firstlings of my heart shall be
> The firstlings of my hand. And even now,
> To crown my thoughts with acts, be it thought and done:
> The castle of Macduff I will surprise;
> Seize upon Fife; give to th' edge o' th' sword
> His wife, his babes, and all unfortunate souls
> That trace him in his line. No boasting like a fool;
> This deed I'll do, before this purpose cool:
> But no more sights! (IV.i.146–55)

For Macbeth, his heirless condition is the source of his insecurity and impotence, his failure to have become a proper safe king; for Shakespeare, it is a symbol for his crippled thought-processes. Both meanings show clearly in this speech at the nadir of Macbeth's progress. With the equivocal word 'firstlings', Macbeth implies that he does indeed have mind-children in his 'heart' and that it is now time their status was confirmed through his 'hand'; his 'thoughts' must be 'crowned with acts'. Their competitors must be wiped out, erased from the market, taken off the screen — 'No more sights!' This is his matching response to the 'crown' of Banquo's ghost: as though this faecal concoction of his own brain evidently imaged a true king (with heirs), against which he must pit himself — equal and replace. In Macbeth's sub-language, 'rubs and botches' in

the institution of kingship are not places where a murder has
been, but places where a murder has not been committed or
completed, acted out. In order for it to be safe, clean and
perfect, the crowning process must be speeded up, made more
efficient ('no boasting'). There must be no gap between impulse
and action: 'be it thought and done'; just as the refrain of the
witches stirring their cauldron is 'I'll do, I'll do and I'll do'.
Shakespeare demonstrates devastatingly how Macbeth's failure
of imagination, under the aegis of omniscience, impairs his
ability to think, and how the language of the political
equivocator slips automatically into that of the fascist
exterminator.

(iv)   Release from the Claustrum

At this point, during the fourth act of the play, the action's
onrush is alleviated through two episodes in which a pause for
thought is attempted: in Lady Macduff's home and in the
monastic court of the English king where the forces of rebellion
are gathering. The knocking at the gate of the castle
immediately after Duncan's murder had branded it a hell of
equivocation; at the same time the approach of Macduff (who
had significantly been left outside at the actual time of the
murder) heralded the beginning of the long process of release
from the claustrum for the mind of Scotland as a whole.
Shakespeare now presents a whole pattern of reciprocal
ambiguous relationships, which both clinch the significance of
the claustrum, and describe a means of release from it. The
interior of the Macduff castle represents the other side of Lady
Macbeth's perverted femininity: it fulfils the promise of the
Macbeth castle as it originally appeared to Duncan and
Banquo, as a 'nest' for fledgling birds, housing the heirs and
features of growth of which Macbeth is barren. Then Macduff's
equivocal knocking at the gates of hell receives a poetic contrast
in the moment of his fleeing from his home, leaving his
femininity (like Macbeth's milk of human kindness)
unprotected and open to destruction. In symbolic terms,
Macduff also is affected by the prevailing air of treachery and
self-seeking 'success': Macbeth pays cynically with his 'eternal
jewel', and Macduff thoughtlessly with the lives of his family,
but when he does so, he is knocking from the outside not

imprisoned inside like Macbeth — a position from which reversal is possible.

When we meet Lady Macduff, her husband has already fled to save himself, and her cousin Rosse is on the point of following him, staying only long enough to try to excuse Macduff's flight as his 'wisdom' — which Lady Macduff, cutting through the equivocation, diagnoses as 'fear':

> Wisdom! to leave his wife, to leave his babes,
> His mansion, and his titles, in a place
> From whence himself does fly? He loves us not:
> He wants the natural touch; for the poor wren,
> The most diminutive of birds, will fight,
> Her young ones in her nest, against the owl.
> All is the fear, and nothing is the love; (IV.ii.6 – 12)

The only apology which Ross can offer on behalf of Macduff, before he escapes himself, is that in these times 'we are traitors,/And do not know ourselves' — just as Macbeth had earlier decided 'not to know himself'. Specifically, it is a not-knowing of their femininity which results in a weak or treacherous masculinity, cowering under the aegis of the perverted witch-mind. Coleridge saw this scene as a relief from the atmosphere of the rest of the play owing to its domesticity, despite the violent ending; it is also a relief owing to its plain-speaking and rejection of equivocation. The conversation between Lady Macduff and her son, on the nature and definition of treachery, is the only intelligent dialogue in the play. Lady Macduff speaks ambiguously, not equivocally, about her husband's unknown fate, leaving the child to interpret her words according to his understanding — which is that his father is not really 'dead' but that if his mother does not weep for him it is a sure sign that she will soon provide him with another (better) father. The murder of the child on the stage in front of its mother parallels Lady Macbeth's image of infanticide, confirming its underlying significance as an attack on imagination and mental growth.

The image is a parallel, but also a reversal and a revelation, in terms of the play's overall drama as a history of one mind. For this time, the meaning of the attack on femininity and the inner world filters through, in the form of an intimate sorrow,

179

to Macduff. Macduff was never actually trapped inside the claustrum — the castle, or its banqueting hall, or the coronation ceremony at Scone, or indeed his own sitting-room; he has always been a figure who hovers on the edges, never there when 'it' happens, the moment of murderous success. Unlike Macbeth he is not prey to Lady Macbeth when faced with the concept of infanticide (indeed, during the second movement of the play, she is incapacitated). Instead, he has placed himself under the strict moral supervision of the English king: submitting himself to a formal testing for treachery by Malcolm, Duncan's son. The English court with its atmosphere of religious sanctity is a type of monastery, dedicated to curing the mysterious disease known as the 'King's Evil' — which implies, in the context of the play, the evil of mindless ambition. For the first time the figure of a 'Doctor' appears. The English court is a place not of creative thinking with the imaginative daring which this entails, but of pious circumspection — never tempted to the 'absolute trust' in political loyalties which had doomed King Duncan. It is a place where the 'painted devils' feared by the 'eye of childhood', and scorned by Lady Macbeth, are taken seriously — writ large in the form of Scotland's politicians. The strange, solemn testing for treachery which Malcolm coldly conducts on Macduff has the air of a religious catechism, rather than of psychological or political realism. Nobody could really believe in the monstrous embodiment of deadly sins which Malcolm portrays as himself. Yet these are the conditions necessary for the 'Macduff' aspect of the mind to receive the message of the latest ravages of 'Macbeth', and the devastation he has wrought on his internal mother-country ('not our mother but our grave'). The test begins with Malcolm reminding Macduff that Macbeth 'hath not touch'd you yet' — that is, has not harmed him intimately. The test is completed when Macduff is 'touch'd' — by the arrival of the news of the murder of his family: a resolution of tension awaited by the audience throughout the scene. Shakespeare thus presents events in such a way that one appears a precondition for the other. Macduff passes the first stage of the test, but is only equipped for the next stage — which indeed goes beyond Malcolm's tutelage — when he recognises his own sinfulness, responsible for the death of his own internal family: 'Sinful

Macduff!/They were all struck for thee'. (IV.iii.224 – 5).
Malcolm tells him to 'dispute it like a man', to which Macduff
replies:

> I shall do so;
> But I must also feel it as a man;

in words which echo and repair Macbeth's earlier attempt to
define his manhood, squashed by Lady Macbeth. At last the
function of 'feeling' has achieved explicit recognition within the
concept of manliness. Macduff is now ready to destroy his
destructive alter-ego, the 'hell-kite' and 'friend of Scotland'; he
too has been a sort of traitor and must return to match himself
against Macbeth face to face:

> front to front,
> Bring thou this fiend of Scotland, and myself. (IV.iii.232 – 3)

In this face-to-face revenge, Macduff finally brings relief to
Macbeth, who is in a state of despairing nullity, oblivious to
hope and fear, imprisoned by the delusory omniscience of the
witch-mind which, he believes, 'knows all mortal consequence'
(V.iii.5). This imprisonment takes the form of his not even
being able to hope that death may be possible, for one who has
'liv'd long enough'; he is trapped in the expectation of an
eternal 'old age' of curses and hatred. Once again, Macduff
knocks on the gate of the claustrum of equivocation, this time
the impregnable castle of Dunsinane, and its victim is released
through death. Macbeth's own 'diseased mind' is mirrored in
that of his 'partner in greatness', his wife, as in her hallucinated
sleepwalking she obsessively relives the original murder.
Unable to dream, her repressed emotions haunt her in the form
of poisonous, undigested elements or 'spots', in the same way
that Macbeth was confronted by the bloody 'crown' of
Banquo's ghost:

> Out, damned spot! ... Hell is murky. Fie, my Lord, Fie!
> A soldier, and afeard? — What need we fear who knows it,
> when none can call our power to accompt? — Yet who would
> have thought the old man to have had so much blood in him?
> ... Here's the smell of the blood still: all the perfumes of
> Arabia will not sweeten this little hand ... To bed, to bed:

there's knocking at the gate. Come, come, come, come, give
me your hand. What's done cannot be undone. To bed, to
bed, to bed. (V.i.34 – 65)

Lady Macbeth never appreciated that hell was an internal
condition rather than a picturebook catechism; her courage was
the spurious type resulting from a lack of imagination. She
could not imagine the consequences of inviting mental 'illness'
to fill her, replacing milk with gall — the witches' brew. When
she chastised Macbeth with 'a little water clears us of this deed
… wash this filthy water from your hand'), she had no
conception of the literalness with which lies as murdered truths
could poison the mind; the 'old man' full of blood now takes
revenge on her 'hand' in the form of another filthy witness. All
her false assumptions and points of thoughtlessness recoil upon
her in the form of the 'damned spots' — murdered feelings
which she hoped to expel or evacuate but cannot mentally
metabolise. Her simplistic belief in 'power' crumbled when she
lost her hold over her husband and she saw 'madness' coming
upon her, its severity equivalent to her own loss of
omnipotence. Shakespeare shows how Lady Macbeth's much
vaunted courage, stoicism, masculinity, is a form of stupidity
which disables her when faced with any real-life events outside
her control; she has no means of working through a reversal of
expectation — just the empty commonsensical refrain 'What's
done cannot be undone'. The delusion of controlling the future
bars her from having any future. Yet in her total isolation, with
the passage to remorse (the key to a future life) still barred, she
nevertheless shows a greater need for communication than
hitherto: the 'little hand' seems part of her body not merely a
machine for holding a knife; 'give me your hand' echoes
Duncan's words to her when he originally entered her castle;
and her invitation 'to bed' suggests following the summons of
the 'knocking at the gate' to a final place of rest.

Macbeth watches her progress intently, recognising though
not sympathising with all the symptoms of his own diseased
inner world — as shown by the uncharacteristic curiosity of his
question to the Doctor: 'Canst thou not minister to a mind
diseas'd?' (V.iii.40). The ambiguity of the term 'minister'
shows Macbeth understands full well that ministry of a 'divine'

or religious character would be required, and that this could not be applied like a drug or a dose of witches' spirit, but would require that 'Therein the patient/Must minister to himself'. He cries, 'Throw physic to the dogs'; and goes to don his armour; but already this is a sign of his beginning to awake from his frozen despair. The knocking at the gate is beginning to penetrate. The first sign occurs when a young servant brings Macbeth news of the approaching English army. In the context of his total mental paralysis, a single awakening spark of fear seems to be objectified in the face of the boy, who Macbeth rounds on contemptuously as a 'cream-fac'd loon', 'lily-liver'd' and 'whey-fac'd', using adjectives for whiteness which remind us of his lost 'milk' of human kindness. Macbeth tells him to 'take his face away' — indicating his disturbance at this potential contact with his own child-self cowering within him, unrecognised. Then, after Lady Macbeth follows the knocking 'to bed', and Macbeth hears the 'cry of women' before her suicide is announced, he seems to waken further from his apathy, saying 'I had almost forgot the taste of fears'. The taste of fear brings a new hope that death may be possible after all, as it was for his wife:

> Tomorrow, and tomorrow, and tomorrow
> Creeps in this petty pace from day to day,
> To the last syllable of recorded time;
> And all our yesterdays have lighted fools
> The way to dusty death. Out, out, brief candle!
> Life's but a walking shadow; a poor player,
> That struts and frets his hour upon the stage,
> And then is heard no more: it is a tale
> Told by an idiot, full of sound and fury,
> Signifying nothing. (V.v.19 – 28)

Macbeth's last soliloquy is an inspired recognition of the meaning of meaninglessness, attained by a poetic translation of the pageant of his wife's sleepwalking upon the stage with her candle, into terms of life's 'walking shadow', just as she shadows his own feeling of non-existence. Shortly after this, Macbeth begins 'to doubt th'equivocation of the fiend/That lies like truth' (V.v.43 – 4), and he searches for signs of his own coming release, starting with Birnam Wood. Superficially it is force that will overcome him, but really it is a personal encounter which has some meaning for him, in which he feels he can confront the witches face to face just as Macduff comes to confront him. For unlike Lady Macbeth's total incomprehension of her symptoms, Macbeth's 'death' is in essence a religious reversal through the person of his alter-ego Macduff. Though Macduff could equivocally be described as 'not born of woman', their relationship is essentially an ambiguous one, two sides of one nature. In effect Macbeth surrenders to him, for he is the stronger fighter and is winning until Macduff identifies himself in a way which allows Macbeth to be slain by the image or the idea rather than by simple physical force. Through this switch or 'death', the mind of Macbeth-Macduff emerges from the claustrum in an atmosphere of avenging piety. The state of Scotland, over which he had attempted to wield omnipotent control with catastrophic consequences, is delivered to Duncan's heir Malcolm, who has been well educated and strictly brought up, but is without his father's childlike naivety. The cloisters of the English court have taught him to observe but not partake of the ways of the world.

Nevertheless there is no guarantee that this will be a deep or permanent solution to Scotland's problems. On the contrary, the values and atmosphere at the end of the play are ominously reminiscent of those at the beginning. Once again Scotland is delivered from the grasp of a bloodthirsty traitor and restored to good King Duncan's line. In the context of battle, the same slogans about honour and valour emerge, to justify pointless deaths: as with old Siward's satisfaction that his son was killed by Macbeth with his wounds on his front: 'He's worth no more;/They say he parted well and paid his score'. Macbeth's head appears on the end of a pole to be the 'show and gaze of the time', just as Macbeth had earlier stuck the head of the 'merciless Macdonwald' on his battlements. To call Macbeth a 'hell-kite' and his wife a 'fiend' may satisfy public accountability, and make everyday and family life possible again for a while, but it does not comprehend the depths of the problem nor does it heal the mind's wounds. The miraculous touch of the English king, shrouded in holy prophecies, serves primarily to mark out an area which Shakespeare will explore most deeply and imaginatively later in the romance plays, in particular *The Winter's Tale*: namely the mind's release from its frozen omnipotence by means of creative internal deities, antithetical to the witches. For the march of Birnam Wood is almost a caricature of the revival of good and green natural forces, a static ideology of its own; and indeed, the 'Doctor' who has a place in both the English and the Scottish courts can only say that he is 'amazed' by Lady Macbeth's condition, but helpless if the patient cannot 'minister to himself'. And a major aspect of Shakespeare's achievement in *Macbeth* consists in his demonstration of how the ''mind diseased' cannot truly be ministered to by the patient's 'self'; it can relinquish dominance to a more healthy part of the self — which is good, kind and moral; but it cannot be transformed, to become a useful and integral part of the personality's developing future, unless a more radical and resilient mode of creative thinking can be established.